Fish

Fish

Contents

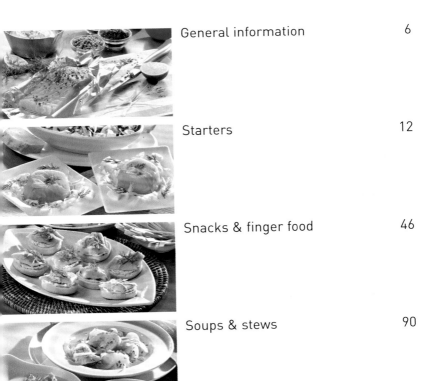

General information   6

Starters   12

Snacks & finger food   46

Soups & stews   90

Light fish dishes 112

Pan-fried dishes 146

Oven-baked dishes 194

Index 238

General information

Freshwater fish

The trout is the best-known and most popular of all the freshwater fish. It is closely related to the salmon family and has delicate flesh, very few bones and is extremely low in calories. Because of their popularity, trout are frequently raised on fish farms. Local relatives of the trout in central and northwest Europe are known as whitefish. Another relative of the trout family, the Arctic char, which has salmon-coloured flesh, is found in alpine lakes.

Carp are the oldest species of farmed fish. They can grow to a great size and weight.

Carp can actually grow to up to 25 kg in weight, although a carp of that size would have very dry flesh. The ideal weight for an edible carp is 1–3 kg.

The freshwater perch has delicious, firm, white flesh with few bones. Its spiny fins make filleting rather difficult. Beginners would be better off starting with ready-to-cook specimens.

The zander is a perfect cross between a pike and a perch: virtually bone-free, firm flesh with a distinctive flavour and well suited to all preparation methods.

The eel, a snake-like, bony fish, found its way into our rivers from the Sargasso Sea. It is caught in rivers and fattened in fish farms. A top-quality eel weighs up to 1.2 kg. Preparing an eel for cooking is quite difficult and requires practice and skill.

Salmon is a migratory fish which, because of its popularity, is raised in fish farms. The most expensive varieties are Pacific silver salmon and king salmon. The flesh of Greenland and Canadian salmon is typically dark red in colour, due to the fact that these salmon feed on prawn shells, which have a high carotene content.

The largest Central European freshwater fish is the catfish. It prefers dark, slow-moving, warm water. The catfish can grow to up to two metres in length and weigh more than 150 kg, at which point it is no longer suitable for consumption. The flesh of smaller specimens (up to 2.5 kg) is firm and has an excellent flavour.

Saltwater fish

Although there are more than 5000 species of freshwater fish, most fish actually live in the ocean. Saltwater fish fall into three main categories: shoaling fish, such as herring and mackerel; round fish, such as cod,

pollock and snappers; and flat fish, such as plaice.

There are approximately 180 species of herring living in our oceans, including sprats, anchovies and sardines.

The mackerel is often eaten smoked as its firm, aromatic flesh makes it ideal for a variety of different preparation methods. It is also so juicy that even novice cooks, who may be less precise in adhering to recommended cooking times, will still be able to produce good results.

The white tuna fish, which can grow up to one metre in length, has light-coloured flesh, which turns pink when cooked. Tuna tastes delicious either grilled or fried.

Red tuna is the largest species of tuna. Its firm flesh, which can be prepared as steaks, turns reddish-brown when cooked.

The best-known species of round fish include the cod, snappers, sea bass, pollock and haddock. These increasingly include whiting, hake and ling.

These are all typical lean fish, which store fat in their liver. This organ is rich in vitamin A and D, and easily processed into cod liver oil. All flat fish have delicate, white, lean flesh, which requires precise cooking times, otherwise it can easily fall apart.

Turbot and sole are the best types of flat fish. Next on the list is halibut, which is usually sold in portions or fillets. It lends itself to all kinds of preparation methods. Smoked halibut is a real delicacy.

Plaice is an extremely delicious and relatively cheap fish. Traditionally, it appears on restaurant menus in May. Its flesh, however, reaches its peak in June. The main fishing area for the flounder, the only North European flat fish species, is the Baltic. The flounder grows to 30–50 cm in size. Its skin is covered in spiny warts, but its flesh is excellent in quality.

Seafood
This category of fish includes all shellfish and crustaceans. Apart from river crabs, they all live in the oceans.

Shellfish
The most common type of shellfish on our menus is mussels: these are bivalve creatures which have a hinge-like mechanism for opening and closing their shells. The most expensive species of shellfish is the oyster, which is traditionally eaten raw. More common are mussels, found in the North Sea, which are popularly cooked in a spicy stock and, like all shellfish, are particularly good if harvested from September to April. The quality is poorer during the warmer months of the year. Their Atlantic and Mediterranean cousins, scallops and clams, are much prized by connoisseurs and may be eaten raw if freshly caught.

Crustaceans
A distinction is made here between long-tailed varieties, such as the lobster, prawns or river crabs, and short-tailed specimens such as edible crabs.

When freshly caught, the shells of these creatures are either light brown or blackish-blue, depending on species. When cooked, the colour changes to light or dark red. The shell of fresh, boiled and unshelled crustaceans should be hard and firm. When cooked, the flesh of these creatures is generally white to pinkish in colour, firm to the bite and has virtually no smell. If the flesh is soft or discoloured, it should not be eaten!

The most characteristic feature of the lobster is its powerful claws. The most delicious part of its flesh is contained in the abdomen and pincers.

Instead of claws, the langoustine has distinctively long antennae. The meat is found only in the rear abdomen which is why you will often find langoustine tails on sale at the fish-mongers. Langoustines and lobsters taste best freshly grilled on the bar-becue or poached in salted water.

The river crab requires very clean water. The majority of river crabs for consumption are imported and available to buy between May and August. Crabs are usually cooked in stock and served with spicy sauces or dips.

Prawns, which also go under the name of shrimps, crevettes or gambas, are found in all the world's oceans in a wide range of species. In commerce, prawns are categorised according to their size and where they are caught: for example, North Sea shrimp and prawns, Greenland and Polar Sea prawns, gambas, king prawns or prawns from Asian waters. Prawns can be prepared in many different ways.

Edible crabs and king crabs are the most common types of short-tailed crabs. The meat is predominantly found in the powerful claws, tail and legs. Generally speaking, the crab meat sold in shops will have come from king crabs.

Starters

Scallop salad
with porcini mushrooms

Serves 4

400 g scallops, with roe,
if desired

salt

pepper

juice of 1 lemon

250 ml fish stock

400 g porcini mushrooms

½ bunch spring onions

3 tbsp butter

1 tbsp freshly chopped dill

1 tbsp white wine vinegar

3 tbsp sunflower oil

1 small iceberg lettuce

1 tbsp chopped chives

Preparation time: approx.
30 minutes (plus cooking time)
Per portion approx. 209 kcal/
878 kJ
13 g P, 14 g F, 9 g CH

1 Scoop the meat from the scallop shells, separate the orange roe from the white meat. Finely chop the scallops and roe, season with salt and pepper and drizzle with lemon juice.

2 Bring the fish stock to a boil in a saucepan. Add the scallops and roe, simmer for a few minutes, then remove from the stock and set aside to cool.

3 Clean and finely chop the porcini mushrooms. Rinse the spring onions and slice into thin rings. Heat the butter in a frying pan and sauté the mushrooms and spring onions together for a few minutes. Season to taste and stir in the chopped dill.

4 To make the salad dressing, season 1 table-spoon of white wine vinegar with salt and pepper, then slowly stir in the oil.

5 Set aside a few lettuce leaves, then shred the rest of the lettuce into small pieces. Line a bowl with the reserved leaves.

6 Place alternating layers of scallop meat, roe, chopped lettuce and mushroom-and-onion mixture on the bed of lettuce, pour the dressing over the top and garnish with chopped chives. Serve with flat bread.

Salmon and prawn
terrines with fresh dill

Serves 4

250 g fresh salmon fillet
salt
freshly ground black pepper
2 sheets leaf gelatine
5 stems dill
2 slices smoked salmon
3½ tbsp mayonnaise
3½ tbsp double cream
juice of ½ lemon
40 g cooked prawns
a little oil

Preparation time: approx.
30 minutes (plus cooking and
chilling time)
Per portion approx. 183 kcal/
768 kJ
17 g P, 11 g F, 4 g CH

1 Preheat the oven to 160 °C (Gas Mark 3). Season the salmon fillet with salt and pepper, wrap in oiled aluminium foil and seal tightly. Place the foil-wrapped salmon in the preheated oven and cook for about 10 minutes.

2 Carefully remove the foil, reserving the cooking juices, then allow the fish to cool. Meanwhile, rinse 4 ramekin dishes or cups in cold water and line each one with a generous amount of cling film, leaving an overhang.

3 Soak the gelatine in cold water. Wash the dill and shake it dry. Place a small sprig of dill on the bottom of each ramekin, then chop the remaining dill and set aside.

4 Place a piece of smoked salmon on top of the dill in each mould. Once cooled, very finely chop or flake the cooked salmon fillet. In a bowl, combine the salmon with the mayonnaise, double cream, fish juices, chopped dill and lemon juice, then stir in the prawns. Squeeze the excess water out of the gelatine and dissolve in a saucepan over a low heat before adding it to the fish mixture.

5 Season the mixture with salt and pepper, then divide equally between the 4 moulds, pressing down gently to remove any air bubbles from the mixture. Cover the mixture with the overhanging cling film. Ideally, leave the terrines to chill and set overnight in the refrigerator. To serve, tip the terrines out onto plates.

Sweet-and-sour
herrings

Serves 4

juice of 2 lemons

150 g sugar

1 tsp whole allspice berries

1 tsp whole white peppercorns

2 bay leaves

6–8 pickled herring fillets, soaked in cold water

1 onion

1 leek

1 bunch freshly chopped dill

Preparation time: approx.
30 minutes (plus marinating time)
Per portion approx. 383 kcal/
1607 kJ
15 g P, 17 g F, 41 g CH

1 Place the lemon juice, 150 ml water, sugar and spices in a saucepan, bring to a boil, then simmer to make a stock. Set aside to cool.

2 Thoroughly drain the pickled herring and cut into slices. Peel and chop the onion, clean the leek and slice thinly into rings.

3 Place alternating layers of onion, leek, herring and dill in a jar or other container. Pour in enough of the cooled stock to cover the herring. Leave to marinate overnight before serving.

Pickled herrings
with tomatoes

Serves 4

6–8 pickled herring fillets,
soaked in water

5 shallots

15 stuffed olives

250 g tomato ketchup

4 tbsp vinegar

4 tbsp sugar

1 tsp salt

1 tsp white pepper

5 tbsp oil

Preparation time: approx.
20 minutes (plus marinating time)
Per portion approx. 403 kcal/
1690 kJ
16 g P, 29 g F, 20 g CH

1 Drain the herrings and cut into small pieces.
Peel and slice the shallots into rings.

2 Place the herrings, shallots and olives in a jar or
other container.

3 In a bowl, combine the ketchup, vinegar, sugar,
salt and pepper. Gradually stir in the oil and mix
well.

4 Cover the herrings with the marinade mixture
and leave to stand for a few hours in the
refrigerator.

Pickled herrings
with aquavit

Serves 4

300 ml vinegar

100 g sugar

½ tbsp white peppercorns

¼ tsp each aniseed and caraway seeds

3 cloves

3 juniper berries

6–8 pickled herrings, soaked in water

3 tbsp aquavit

1 tsp finely chopped lemon peel

Preparation time: approx. 15 minutes (plus marinating time)
Per portion approx. 320 kcal/ 1344 kJ
14 g P, 17 g F, 27 g CH

1 In a saucepan, bring the vinegar, sugar and spices to a boil, then set the resulting stock aside to cool.

2 Peel and slice the onions into thin rings. Drain the herrings and cut into pieces.

3 Place alternating layers of herring and onion rings in a jar or similar container. Add the aquavit and lemon peel to the cooking stock, then pour over the herrings. Chill in the refrigerator for several hours.

Pickled herrings
with ginger

Serves 4

4 fresh herring
500 ml vinegar
150 g sugar
250 g red onions
100 g carrots
25 g horseradish root
15 g fresh ginger root
1½ tsp allspice berries
2 tsp mustard seeds
3 bay leaves

Preparation time: approx.
50 minutes (plus soaking and
marinating time)
Per portion approx. 448 kcal/
1879 kJ
22 g P, 26 g F, 31 g CH

1 Cut the herring fillets off the bone, leaving the backbone in place and soak in cold water overnight. Rinse well and cut into approx. 2-cm lengths.

2 In a saucepan, bring the vinegar and sugar to a boil. Simmer gently, stirring until the sugar is completely dissolved. Allow the liquid to cool.

3 Peel and thinly slice the onions and carrots. Peel and finely grate the horseradish and ginger.

4 Place alternating layers of the above ingredients in a jar or similar container, inserting the spices and bay leaves at intervals. Finally, pour in the cooled liquid, cover and leave to chill in the refrigerator for several days. This herring appetiser tastes delicious served with bread or potato salad.

Prawns
in spicy sauce

Serves 4

800 g large, unpeeled
prawn tails

salt

2 garlic cloves

1 piece fresh ginger (1 cm)

3 tbsp soy sauce

1 tbsp rice wine

2 tsp sugar

pepper

1 tsp cornstarch

4 spring onions

4 tbsp corn oil

2 tbsp *kecap manis*

50 ml fish stock

Preparation time: approx.
45 minutes (plus cooking time)
Per portion approx. 278 kcal/
1166 kJ
41 g P, 9 g F, 8 g CH

1 Wash and peel the prawns leaving the tail on. De-vein the prawns, pat dry and rub with salt. Leave to stand for 10 minutes.

2 Peel and very finely chop the garlic and ginger. Mix the ginger with soy sauce, rice wine, sugar and pepper. Mix the cornstarch with a little water to form a smooth paste. Clean and wash the spring onions, then cut diagonally into thin slices.

3 Rub a little oil around the inside of a wok, then add the remaining oil and heat. Fry the garlic cloves in the wok with a little salt. Add the prawns and fry until they turn pink, turning occasionally.

4 Add the ginger and soy sauce, the *kecap manis* and fish stock. Simmer all the ingredients for 3 minutes. Add the cornstarch paste and bring to a boil, stirring continuously, until the liquid begins to thicken. Serve the prawns garnished with spring onions.

Rhenish-style mussels

Serves 4

2 kg mussels

2–3 onions

1–2 carrots

¼ celeriac

½ leek

½ bunch parsley

4 juniper berries

8 black peppercorns

2 bay leaves

salt

0.5 l dry white wine

Preparation time: approx.
25 minutes (plus cooking time)
Per portion approx. 770 kcal/
3234 kJ
103 g P, 15 g F, 50 g CH

1 Thoroughly scrub the mussels clean in water and rinse thoroughly several times until all traces of sand are removed. Remove any mussels which are not tightly closed. Peel and finely dice the onions. Similarly, peel, wash and finely dice the carrots and celeriac. Clean and rinse the leek, then slice into thin rings. Wash the parsley.

2 Next, add the above ingredients to a saucepan together with the crushed juniper berries, the peppercorns, bay leaves, salt and wine. Add the mussels and cover with water.

3 Cook all the ingredients until the mussels have opened, discarding any that have failed to open. Remove from the heat and allow to stand for 5 minutes. To serve, divide the mussels between 4 deep plates and cover each portion with some of the liquid. This dish goes well with thick, buttered slices of dark rye or wholemeal bread.

Seafood salad
with cashew nuts

Serves 4

750 g mixed seafood, ready
to cook (e.g. small squid,
prawns and fillets of various
saltwater fish)

3 garlic cloves

1 small green pepper

1 small red pepper

3–4 stems basil

4 tbsp oil

2 tsp roasted *Naam Prik Pao*
chilli paste (available from
most Asian food stores)

2 tbsp fish sauce

approx. 2 tbsp brown sugar

30 g unsalted cashew nuts

Preparation time: approx.
20 minutes (plus cooking time)
Per portion approx. 260 kcal/
1092 kJ
32 g P, 10 g F, 9 g CH

1 Wash the seafood and pat dry. Cut into bite-sized chunks. Cut the squid into small pieces and score a cross in each piece, which will cause it to roll up into an attractive shape. Cube the fish fillets.

2 Peel and finely dice the garlic. Wash and halve the peppers, remove the stalks and seeds and slice into strips. Wash the basil, shake it dry and tear the leaves off the stalks.

3 Heat the oil gently in a frying pan and fry the garlic until golden brown. Stir in the chilli paste and add the strips of pepper.

4 Add the various seafood ingredients, fish sauce and sugar, then cover and cook all the ingredients over a moderate heat for about 5 minutes. Add more fish sauce to taste and stir in the fresh basil.

5 Fry the cashew nuts in a dry frying pan without fat until golden brown. Sprinkle these over the salad and serve whilst still warm but not hot.

Herring salad
with beetroot

Serves 4

2 salted herrings
4 potatoes
1 beetroot
2 apples
2 onions
1–2 pickled gherkins
1 tsp mustard
3 tbsp vinegar
2 tbsp oil
2–3 tbsp sour cream
sugar to taste

Preparation time: approx.
45 minutes (plus soaking time)
Per portion approx. 195 kcal/
820 kJ
15 g P, 12 g F, 6 g CH

1 Soak the herrings in cold water for about 24 hours, then pat dry. Remove the bones from the fish, fillet and cut into fine strips.

2 Wash the potatoes and cook for 20 minutes. Drain, then allow to cool completely before peeling and dicing. Wash the beetroot, cook in salted water for 20 minutes, then drain and allow to cool. Peel and dice the beetroot.

3 Wash, peel, core and dice the apples. Peel the onions and slice into rings. Finely slice the pickled gherkins. Place all the ingredients in a bowl.

4 Make a marinade by mixing together the mustard, vinegar, oil and sour cream and pour this over the ingredients in the bowl. If necessary, add a little sugar to the herring salad if it is still too sour.

Smoked salmon rolls
with carrot spirals

Serves 4

8 slices smoked salmon,
30 g each

1 tbsp mustard

1 tbsp honey

freshly ground pepper

1 bunch dill

4 iceberg lettuce leaves

1 carrot

1 piece fresh horseradish
root (approx. 1 cm)

1 tbsp lemon juice

cress and lemon slices
to garnish

Preparation time: approx.
15 minutes
Per portion approx. 131 kcal/
551 kJ
13 g P, 4 g F, 10 g CH

1 Spread out the salmon slices on a work surface. In a bowl, combine the mustard and honey, seasoning with a little pepper.

2 Wash the dill, shake off any excess water, then finely chop. Stir the dill into the mustard-and-honey mixture. Spread this over the salmon slices.

3 Wash and dry the lettuce leaves, remove the thick rib down the centre and cut the leaves in half lengthwise. Arrange the strips of lettuce on the salmon slices and roll up.

4 Clean and wash the carrot, then, using a sharp potato peeler, peel the carrot into thin spirals. Divide the carrot spirals between 4 plates, then arrange the salmon rolls on top.

5 Sprinkle with freshly grated horseradish, then drizzle lemon juice over all the ingredients. Garnish with cress and lemon slices before serving.

Tip

When preparing the mustard and honey cream, make double the quantity. If stored in a firmly sealed container, the cream will keep for at least 1 week in the refrigerator.

Marinated salmon

Serves 4

3 bunches dill

4 tbsp salt

5 tbsp sugar

1 kg salmon, boned and cut into 2 fillets, ready to cook, with the skin left on

1 tbsp peppercorns

mustard seeds to taste

allspice berries to taste

Preparation time: approx.
20 minutes (plus marinating time)
Per portion approx. 278 kcal/
1165 kJ
35 g P, 12 g F, 7 g CH

1 Finely chop the dill. Combine the salt and sugar in a bowl. Spread half the dill over a large, flat platter. Place one of the salmon fillets, skin side facing down, on the layer of dill.

2 Rub half the sugar-and-salt mixture into the salmon. Sprinkle with a little ground pepper, the mustard seeds and allspice berries.

3 Repeat the process with the other salmon fillet, then sandwich the two halves back together (with the skin on the outside). Cover with foil and chill in the refrigerator for 3 days, turning several times.

4 Remove the skin and spices from the marinated salmon and cut into thin slices. Served with crispbread, this also makes an ideal snack.

Tuna carpaccio
with sherry

Serves 4

350 g fresh tuna

1 shallot

2 tbsp extra virgin olive oil

2 tbsp dry sherry

1 tsp sherry vinegar

salt

black pepper

3 tsp small capers

Preparation time: approx.
10 minutes (plus freezing time)
Per portion approx. 280 kcal/
1176 kJ
20 g P, 20 g F, 3 g CH

1 Wash and dry the tuna fish, wrap in aluminium foil and place in the freezer for approx. 2 hours to make it easier to slice.

2 Peel and finely dice the shallot. Combine the olive oil, sherry, sherry vinegar, salt and pepper, mixing vigorously. Stir in the shallot and drained capers.

3 Slice the semi-frozen tuna into wafer-thin slices. Arrange these on four plates and drizzle the sauce over the top. Serve with toasted baguette and dry sherry.

Lobster salad
with mint

Serves 4

1 lobster (approx. 1 kg)
400 g water melon
300 g honeydew melon
juice of 1 lemon
2 tbsp acacia honey
6 mint leaves
1 tbsp sugar
3 tbsp grape seed oil
50 g unsalted cashew nuts

Preparation time: approx.
45 minutes
Per portion approx. 547 kcal/
2300 kJ
43 g P, 25 g F, 27 g CH

1 Place the lobster in boiling water and cook for approx. 5 minutes. Next, crack open the shell and claws, scoop out the meat and cut into strips.

2 Scoop out balls of fruit using a melon scoop.

3 Mix the lemon juice with honey, mint, sugar and oil.

4 Arrange the melon balls and lobster decoratively on a plate and drizzle with sauce. Garnish with the cashew nuts.

Sole roulades
with raisins

Serves 4

4 sole fillets
salt
pepper
½ unwaxed orange
½ unwaxed lemon
2 tbsp raisins
3 spring onions
4–6 tbsp olive oil

Preparation time: approx.
15 minutes (plus marinating and
baking time)
Per portion approx. 230 kcal/
966 kJ
27 g P, 7 g F, 12 g CH

1 Using a sharp knife, make several diagonal incisions in the skin side of each fillet. Season with salt and pepper. With the skin on the inside, roll up the fillets and place side by side in a casserole dish, tighly packed together.

2 Wash the orange and lemon in hot water, then dry and grate the peel. Squeeze the juice out of the orange and lemon and mix with the citrus zest, raisins and a little pepper. Pour the resulting marinade over the fillets.

3 Clean and wash the spring onions, then slice diagonally into thin rings. Sprinkle these over the fish roulades. Drizzle with olive oil, cover and marinate overnight in the refrigerator.

4 Next day, preheat the oven to 250 °C (Gas Mark 9) and bake the sole roulades for approx. 20 minutes. Serve warm with ciabatta or wild rice.

Tip

The sole is a member of the flat fish family and therefore provides 4 fillets, 2 from the upper side and 2 from the underside of the fish.

Marinated herring nibbles
with paprika

Serves 4

4 marinated herring fillets, lightly salted

¼ yellow pepper

1 shallot

1 tbsp natural yoghurt

2 tbsp sour cream

1 tbsp chilli sauce

1–2 tsp lemon juice

salt

pepper

sugar

½ punnet cress

2 tbsp butter

4 slices white bread

Preparation time: approx. 15 minutes (plus frying time)
Per portion approx. 360 kcal/ 1512 kJ
22 g P, 26 g F, 10 g CH

1 Give the herring fillets a quick rinse, pat dry and cut into bite-sized chunks. Wash and finely dice the bell pepper. Peel the shallot and cut into fine rings. Mix the diced pepper and shallot rings with the yoghurt, sour cream and chilli sauce. Flavour the sauce with lemon juice, salt, pepper and sugar, to taste.

2 Wash the cress and shake dry. Melt the butter in a frying pan until it begins to bubble. Fry the bread on both sides until golden brown. Remove from the pan and leave to cool.

3 Cut the fried bread into triangles and spread with a small amount of sauce. Arrange pieces of herring on each triangle and top with the remaining sauce. Garnish with cress before serving.

Snacks & finger food

Salmon-stuffed
vine leaves

Serves 4

36 preserved vine leaves
300 g smoked salmon
1 red chilli pepper
3 tbsp creamed horseradish
2 tbsp curry powder
600 g cream cheese
lemon pepper
300 g herring fillets
3 tbsp preserved peppers
(various colours)
1 green chilli pepper
salt
ground paprika

Preparation time approx.
35 minutes (plus chilling time)
Per portion approx. 732 kcal/
3076 kJ
45 g P, 72 g F, 6 g CH

1 Thoroughly rinse the vine leaves, then place in ice-cold water for a few minutes. Spread them out on a work surface and cut off the stems. Finely chop the salmon.

2 Wash the red chilli pepper, cut in half lengthwise, remove the seeds, then dice. Mix the diced chilli with the salmon, creamed horseradish, curry powder and 300 g cream cheese. Season to taste with lemon pepper. Chop the herring fillets into small pieces.

3 Drain the preserved peppers in a sieve, then finely dice. Wash the green chilli pepper, cut it in half lengthwise, then dice.

4 Mix the herring fillets, peppers and diced chillis with the remaining cream cheese. Season to taste with salt and paprika.

5 Spoon the salmon-and-cheese mixture onto half the vine leaves and top the remaining half with the herring-and-cheese filling. Fold in the ends and roll up the leaves. Chill in the refrigerator for approx. 1 hour before serving.

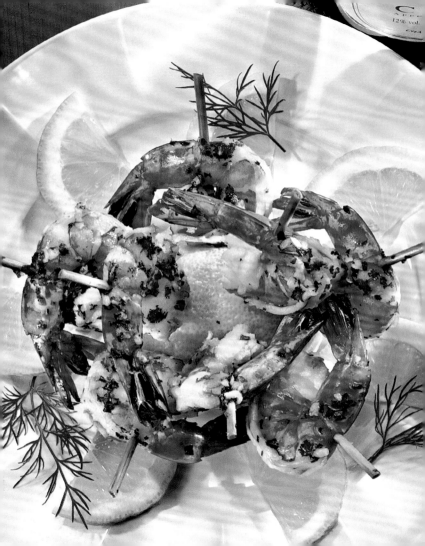

Garlic
prawn kebabs

Serves 4

5 garlic cloves
½ bunch parsley
24 large, peeled prawns
3 tbsp olive oil
1 dried red chilli pepper
100 ml vegetable stock

Preparation time: approx.
10 minutes (plus cooking time)
Per portion approx. 695 kcal/
2919 kJ
122 g P, 20 g F, 6 g CH

1 Preheat the oven to 200 °C (Gas Mark 6). Peel and finely chop the garlic. Wash the parsley, shake it dry and chop finely. Wash and drain the prawns, de-vein them first, if necessary.

2 Heat the oil in a frying pan and gently fry the garlic. Crumble the chilli pepper, then add to the garlic. Add the parsley and continue to fry for 2 minutes, stirring constantly.

3 Add the prawns and pour in the vegetable stock. Cook in the oven for about 15 minutes. Spear each prawn on a wooden cocktail stick and serve in the resulting sauce. Crusty white bread makes a perfect accompaniment to this dish.

Salmon

with dill and mustard sauce

Serves 4

5 tbsp mild mustard

4 tbsp vinegar

3 tbsp sugar

1 tsp salt

½ tsp pepper

200 ml cooking oil

2 bunches freshly
chopped dill

300 g marinated salmon
(see recipe on page 36)

Preparation time: approx.
15 minutes
Per portion approx. 320 kcal/
1344 kJ
29 g P, 23 g F, 1 g CH

1 Combine the mustard, vinegar, sugar and seasoning in a bowl.

2 Mix together thoroughly until the sugar has completely dissolved.

3 Add the oil, a few drops at a time, stirring vigorously the whole time. Finally, stir in the dill and place the sauce in the refrigerator until required. Serve the sauce as an accompaniment to the marinated salmon.

Salmon

with vinaigrette dressing

Serves 4

1 onion
½ bunch mixed herbs
2 tbsp white wine vinegar
2 tbsp olive oil
salt
pepper
300 g marinated salmon
(see recipe on page 36)

Preparation time: approx.
20 minutes
Per portion approx. 258 kcal/
1082 kJ
28 g P, 16 g F, 1 g CH

1 Chop the onion as finely as possible. Wash the herbs and shake them dry. Then, either chop them very finely by hand or in an electric food processer.

2 Combine the vinegar, oil, onion and herbs and season with salt and pepper.

3 Serve slices of marinated salmon with the vinaigrette dressing.

Salmon

with honey-and-dill sauce

Serves 4

1 bunch dill

2 egg yolks

2 tbsp sugar

6 tsp medium-hot mustard

6 tsp clear honey

2 tbsp double cream

2 tbsp lemon juice

salt

pepper

300 g marinated salmon
(see recipe on page 36)

Preparation time: approx.
10 minutes
Per portion approx. 318 kcal/
1333 kJ
31 g P, 14 g F, 16 g CH

1 Finely chop the fresh dill. Beat the egg yolks well, then add the sugar, mustard, honey and cream.

2 Add enough lemon juice to the sauce to achieve the desired sweet-and-sour flavour. Season with salt and pepper to taste.

3 Finally, stir in the dill and refrigerate the sauce until required. Serve as an accompaniment to slices of marinated salmon.

Sashimi

with soy sauce

Serves 4

250 g salmon or haddock, freshly caught

250 g tuna, freshly caught

1 small, white radish

1 carrot

1 tbsp wasabi powder

100 ml Japanese soy sauce

75 ml semi-dry mirin or sherry

Preparation time: approx. 30 minutes
Per portion approx. 268 kcal/ 1123 kJ
27 g P, 14 g F, 3 g CH

1 Skin and fillet the fish, removing all the bones, then wash thoroughly and pat dry. Using a very sharp knife, cut the prepared salmon or haddock fillets into wafer-thin slices.

2 Using a very sharp knife, cut the tuna fish into small chunks. Arrange the diced tuna and salmon or haddock slices on 4 plates.

3 Clean and peel the radish and carrot, then slice into thin strips and divide the vegetable strips between the 4 plates.

4 Mix the wasabi powder into a smooth paste with a few drops of water, then place a portion on each plate.

5 Combine the soy sauce with the mirin or sherry, then divide between 4 small bowls and place a small bowl with sauce on each plate.

Grilled scallops

Serves 4

2–3 stems tarragon
½ bunch flat-leaf parsley
2 garlic cloves
3 shallots
3 tbsp olive oil
salt
freshly ground pepper
20 scallops, removed from
their shells
400 g firm, white fish fillet
1 tbsp chopped chives

Preparation time: approx.
15 minutes (plus marinating and
frying time)
Per portion approx. 239 kcal/
1002 kJ
32 g P, 8 g F, 9 g CH

1 Wash the herbs and shake them dry, then finely chop. Peel the garlic and shallots. Finely chop the shallots, crush the garlic and mix the two together. Stir the herbs, shallots and garlic into the olive oil, then season with salt and pepper.

2 Add the scallops to the oil mixture. Divide the fish fillets into bite-sized chunks and add to the scallops and oil. Cover and marinate in the refrigerator for at least 1 hour.

3 Remove the scallops and fish from the marinade and drain on kitchen towel. Spear alternating pieces of fish and scallops onto kebab skewers and grill for about 5 minutes, turning the skewers after approx. 2 minutes. Arrange the kebabs on a platter to serve and sprinkle with chopped chives to garnish.

Mussel vol-au-vents

Serves 8

8 puff pastry cases
(vol-au-vents)
500–750 g cod fillets
lemon juice
salt
250 ml fish stock
125 ml dry white wine
100 g button mushrooms
40 g butter
500 g mussels
1 tbsp flour
100 g crab meat
pepper
1 egg yolk
3 tbsp cream

Preparation time: approx.
30 minutes (plus cooking and
baking time)
Per vol-au-vent approx.
277 kcal/1165 kJ
22 g P, 15 g F, 10 g CH

1 Clean the fish fillets, sprinkle with lemon juice and season with salt.

2 Bring the fish stock to a boil in a saucepan, stir in the white wine and poach the fish fillets in the stock for about 8 minutes.

3 Clean the mushrooms, slice, then fry gently in a small amount of butter. Thoroughly clean the mussels, boil in salted water and scoop the meat from the shell.

4 Heat the mussels in butter, sprinkle with flour and pour in the fish stock. Simmer gently for 10–12 minutes.

5 Remove the fish from the stock and drain. Roughly chop the fish into pieces and mix with the crab meat. Season with salt and pepper, then add the egg yolk and cream.

6 Bake the puff pastry cases in the oven, according to the instructions on the packet, fill each with a portion of the fish filling and serve.

Asparagus and zander
in puff pastry

Serves 4

200 g frozen puff pastry
500 g green asparagus
salt
1 egg yolk
200 g fillet of zander
or turbot
75 ml dry white wine
1 chopped shallot
200 g butter
pepper
1 tbsp lemon juice
2 tbsp crème fraîche
1 bunch chervil
flour for dusting

Preparation time: approx.
20 minutes (plus cooking and
baking time)
Per portion approx. 480 kcal/
2016 kJ
15 g P, 39 g F, 18 g CH

1 Defrost the puff pastry. Pre-heat the oven to 225 °C (Gas Mark 7–8). Peel the lower section of the asparagus and cut off the stalk end. Cook in salted water for approx. 8 minutes until the asparagus is just firm to the bite. Remove from the saucepan and drain, retaining some of the cooking water. Measure out 75 ml of the asparagus water and set aside.

2 Dust a work surface with flour, then roll out the puff pastry to a thickness of approx. 5 mm. Cut into 4 equal squares, brush with beaten egg yolk and bake in the preheated oven for approx. 5–8 minutes until golden brown.

3 Wash the fish and pat dry, cut into 4 portions and steam for 4–5 minutes until cooked through. Bring the asparagus cooking water to a boil with the wine and shallot and simmer until the liquid is reduced by half. Stir in the cold butter, a few flakes at a time.

4 Season with pepper, salt and lemon juice to taste but do not cook any further. Fold in the crème fraîche. Wash the chervil, shake it dry, then tear off the leaves and add to the sauce.

5 Cut the puff pastry squares in half horizontally. Cut the asparagus stems in half and place on the puff pastry base. Then, add a piece of fish, drizzle with sauce and replace the puff pastry lid.

Trout tartare
on rye bread

Serves 4

4 smoked trout fillets
2 celery sticks
½ red pepper
1 gherkin
100 g crème fraîche
salt
pepper
rye bread
butter
½ bunch dill

Preparation time: approx.
20 minutes
Per portion approx. 258 kcal/
1082 kJ
27 g P, 13 g F, 8 g CH

1 Skin the trout fillets and cut into small pieces. Clean and wash the celery, then chop very finely. Wash, clean, de-seed and very finely chop the red pepper. Finely chop the gherkin.

2 Mix the trout with the finely chopped celery, gherkin and pepper. Stir in the crème fraîche and add salt and pepper to taste.

3 Butter slices of rye bread and top each one with the trout-and-celery tartare. Wash the dill, shake it dry, then top each slice with a little sprig of dill before serving.

Scones

with trout fillet

Serves 4

175 g flour
1½ tsp baking powder
pinch of salt
50 g butter
1 egg
approx. 3 tbsp cream
4–6 stems fresh dill
150 ml sour cream
¾ tbsp freshly grated
horseradish root
175 g smoked trout fillet
freshly ground black pepper
trout caviar to garnish
flour for dusting

Preparation time: approx.
25 minutes (plus baking time)
Per portion approx. 285 kcal/
1197 kJ
15 g P, 10 g F, 33 g CH

1 Preheat the oven to 200 °C (Gas Mark 6). Combine the flour, baking powder and salt. Cut the butter into small pieces, add to the flour mixture along with the lightly beaten egg. Add just enough cream to knead into a smooth dough. Lightly dust a work surface with flour and roll out the dough to a thickness of approx. 2 cm. Cut out small rounds.

2 Place the scones on a baking sheet lined with baking paper and bake in the oven for approx. 8–10 minutes until golden brown. Remove from the oven, cover with a cloth and allow to cool.

3 Wash the dill, shake dry, reserve a small amount for garnishing purposes, then finely chop the rest. Cut the scones in half horizontally. Mix the sour cream with the grated horseradish and blend in the finely chopped dill. Spread this mixture over the scones.

4 Divide the trout fillet into approx. 20 portions, place on the halved scones, then sprinkle with pepper. Garnish with caviar and the remaining dill to serve.

Grilled oysters

Serves 4

16 oysters
250 g chard
1 bunch spring onions
3 garlic cloves
300 g butter
4 tbsp vegetable stock
salt
pepper
3 egg yolks
125 ml dry white wine
2 sprigs tarragon
2 sprigs chervil

Preparation time: approx.
50 minutes
Per portion approx. 788 kcal/
3311 kJ
15 g P, 68 g F, 14 g CH

1 Open up the oysters and scoop out the flesh. Clean, wash and dry the chard, and slice into thin strips.

2 Clean, wash and dry the spring onions, and slice into thin rings. Peel and finely chop the garlic cloves.

3 Heat 2 tablespoons of butter in a frying pan and gently fry the spring onions and garlic. Add the chard, cook for a few more minutes, then pour in the vegetable stock. Season with salt and pepper, cover and cook for approx. 5 minutes.

4 Grease a heatproof baking dish with 1 tablespoon of butter. Whisk the egg yolk and white wine together in a hot bain-marie until frothy. Whisk 250 g butter, cut into flakes, into the egg mixture.

5 Wash, dry and finely chop the herbs, then add to the Béarnaise sauce, season with salt and pepper. Fill the empty oyster shells with the vegetable mixture.

6 Top each one with an oyster, then drizzle sauce over the top. Cook the oysters under the grill until the sauce turns golden brown.

Prawn parcels
with hoisin sauce

Serves 4

400 g peeled prawns
1 tsp cornstarch
150 g button mushrooms
4 spring onions
1 piece fresh ginger root (approx. 2 cm)
3 garlic cloves
1 chopped red chilli pepper
2 tbsp oil
1 tbsp sesame oil
salt
pepper
1 tbsp soy sauce
2 tbsp rice wine or sherry
pinch of sugar
2 tbsp chopped coriander or parsley
1 packet rice paper sheets
125 g soy bean sprouts, drained
5 tbsp hoisin sauce
5 tbsp freshly squeezed orange juice

Preparation time: approx. 30 minutes
Per portion approx. 239 kcal/ 1004 kJ
24 g P, 11 g F, 9 g CH

1 Blanch the prawns in boiling water, drain, plunge in cold water, then pat dry. Cut in half lengthwise, de-vein, then rub with cornstarch.

2 Clean the mushrooms, then cut into strips. Clean and wash the spring onions. Slice the white parts into thin rings and chop the green sections. Peel and finely chop the ginger and garlic, then mix all the ingredients with the chilli pepper.

3 Heat 1 tablespoon of oil in a frying pan. Mix half the prawns with half the vegetable mixture and stir in a little sesame oil, then season with salt and pepper. Cook for 4 minutes, stirring constantly, then season with soy sauce, rice wine, sugar and coriander. Remove from the pan and repeat the process with the other half of the prawns.

4 Dip the rice paper sheets one by one in cold water, then spread them out on a work surface. Leave the rice papers until they turn milky. Take 2 sheets at a time and place one on top of the other, then top with a spoonful of the prawn-and-vegetable mixture. Divide the bean sprouts between the rice paper sheets, then roll them up. Mix the hoisin sauce and orange juice together. Dip each prawn parcel in the sauce before eating.

Two-fish terrine

Serves 4

450 g salmon fillet
250 g asparagus
400 g sea bass
1 egg
300 ml cream
salt
pepper
1 tbsp freshly chopped chervil
3 tbsp freshly chopped dill
3 tbsp freshly chopped parsley
200 g sour cream
100 g mayonnaise
2 tbsp lemon juice

Preparation time: approx.
30 minutes (plus cooking and baking time)
Per portion approx. 733 kcal/
3076 kJ
47 g P, 58 g F, 7 g CH

1 Very finely dice the salmon fillet. Clean and peel the asparagus, cut off the woody end, then cut into pieces. Cook the asparagus in salted water for approx. 15 minutes.

2 Mince the sea bass fillet in a food processor, then mix the fish with the egg, cream, salt and pepper. Fold the chervil, diced salmon and asparagus into the mixture. Preheat the oven to 175 °C (Gas Mark 4).

3 Grease the inside of a terrine mould and tip in the fish mixture. Level off the surface using a palette knife and cover with aluminium foil. Place the terrine in a bain-marie and bake in the oven for about 1 hour.

4 Once the terrine is cooked, allow it to cool completely before tipping it out of the mould and slicing.

5 To make the sauce, blend the remaining ingredients together and serve as an accompaniment.

Salmon

stuffed with crab meat

Serves 4

12 lettuce leaves (e.g. green salad, radicchio or lollo rosso)

150 ml cream

1 tbsp lemon juice

4 tsp horseradish (from a jar)

350 g crab meat

salt

pepper

8 slices smoked salmon

a few sprigs of dill

Preparation time: approx. 20 minutes
Per portion approx. 240 kcal/ 1009 kJ
25 g P, 15 g F, 3 g CH

1 Wash the lettuce leaves, pat dry, then divide between 4 plates.

2 Whisk the cream until stiff, flavour with lemon juice to taste, then mix with the horseradish.

3 Fold the crab meat into the horseradish cream and season with salt and pepper.

4 Spoon the crab meat mixture onto the 8 salmon slices and roll up. Secure with wooden cocktail sticks. Arrange on plates and garnish with dill.

Nigiri sushi
with tuna and caviar

Serves 4

125 g sushi rice
1 tbsp rice vinegar
1 tbsp sugar
½ tsp salt
2 tsp wasabi powder
1 tbsp rice wine (mirin)
small amount of
vinegar water
approx. 50 g extremely fresh
fish fillet (e.g. tuna or
mackerel)
½ nori leaf
3–4 tbsp trout or salmon
caviar, or sea urchin roe
soy sauce to serve

Preparation time: approx.
25 minutes (plus cooking and
chilling time)
Per portion approx. 145 kcal/
608 kJ
6 g P, 2 g F, 26 g CH

1 Wash and drain the rice, then bring to a boil in 150 ml water and simmer for 10 minutes. Leave to stand in the steam in the saucepan for a further 15 minutes. Bring the rice vinegar, sugar and salt to a boil, allow to cool, then mix with the rice. Leave the rice to cool completely.

2 Mix the wasabi powder with 2 teaspoons of water and the mirin. Moisten your hands with vinegar water, then, taking 1 tablespoon of rice at a time, shape the rice into about 12 ovals.

3 Cut the fish fillet diagonally into 6 slices, then spread half the wasabi mixture on one side of each fish slice. Taking 1 slice of fish at a time in the left hand, lay a rice ball on top and press down firmly. Turn the sushi over and press into a neat, oval shape.

4 Toast the nori leaf briefly on one side in a fat-free frying pan, then cut into strips approx. 3–4 cm wide and spread with the remaining wasabi mixture. Wrap the remaining rice balls in a strip of nori leaf so that the leaf drapes over the top.

5 Gently press down the rice within and fill the extra space thereby created with caviar or roe. Nigiri sushi should always be served in pairs, accompanied by soy sauce.

Eel kebabs
with spicy dressing

Serves 4

1½ kg skinned eels, ready to cook

approx. 20 fresh bay leaves

100 ml wine vinegar

2 tbsp oil

¼ tsp ground pepper

¼ tsp ground cloves

¼ tsp ground cinnamon

¼ tsp ground ginger

1 sprig rosemary

3 oranges

2 lemons

2–3 tbsp pomegranate juice

salt

ginger

cardamom

Preparation time: approx.
15 minutes (plus grilling time)
Per portion approx. 855 kcal/
3591 kJ
40 g P, 68 g F, 68 g CH

1 Cut the skinned eels into chunks and spear on skewers with a bay leaf between each piece.

2 Combine the vinegar, oil, pepper, cloves, cinnamon and ginger, and add the sprig of rosemary.

3 Squeeze the juice from the oranges and lemons and mix with the pomegranate juice.

4 Slowly grill the kebabs over a barbecue. Using the sprig of rosemary, keep brushing the oil-and-vinegar mixture over the kebabs.

5 Arrange the pieces of cooked eel in a deep serving dish and pour the fruit juice mixture over the top. Sprinkle with salt, ginger and cardamom and serve warm. Freshly baked bread makes a perfect accompaniment to this dish.

Fish and seafood
kebabs

Serves 4

175 g squid, ready to cook

12 peeled prawns

200 g salmon fillet

3 tbsp flour

75 ml soy sauce

75 ml dry white wine

1 piece fresh ginger root
(approx. 1 cm)

2 tbsp oil

lemon wedges for garnish

Preparation time approx.
20 minutes
Per portion approx. 455 kcal/
1911 kJ
79 g P, 10 g F, 10 g CH

1 Soak 8 wooden skewers in cold water. Carefully wash the squid and cut into bite-sized pieces. De-vein the prawns, if necessary, wash and drain.

2 Cut the salmon fillet into bite-sized pieces. Load the kebabs with alternating pieces of squid, prawns and salmon chunks, and toss in flour.

3 Pour the soy sauce and wine into a saucepan. Peel the ginger and grate into the saucepan. Bring to a boil.

4 Heat 2 tablespoons of oil in a frying pan. Fry the kebabs over a moderate heat on both sides for about 3–5 minutes until golden brown. Add the sauce and allow to caramelise in the frying pan. Serve the kebabs with sauce and lemon wedges.

Tip

Any type of fish or seafood can be used for these kebabs. Small squids also taste really good.

Savoy cabbage roulades
with langoustines

Serves 4

16–18 langoustines
(also known as Dublin Bay
prawns)

salt

pepper

2 tbsp chopped tarragon

50 g diced carrots

50 g leeks, sliced into rings

50 g diced kohlrabi

4 savoy cabbage leaves

2 tbsp melted butter

1 chopped shallot

1 diced small mango

75 g butter

1 tbsp curry powder

2 tbsp Noilly Prat (Vermouth)

1 tbsp white port wine

125 ml fish stock

125 ml cream

small amount of lime juice

1 tbsp olive oil

Preparation time approx.
25 minutes (plus cooking time)
Per portion 365 kcal/1533 kJ
34 g P, 22g F, 9 g CH

1 Peel the langoustines, leaving the tail fins on 4 of them. De-vein and wash. Dice all the langoustines apart from the 4 with tails, season with salt, pepper and tarragon.

2 Blanch all the diced vegetables and leek rings for 1 minute in boiling, salted water, plunge in cold water, drain and mix with the diced langoustines. Similarly, blanch the savoy cabbage leaves for 2 minutes, then plunge in cold water and drain.

3 Sprinkle the cabbage leaves with salt, then spoon some of the mixture into the centre of each leaf. Roll up the leaves into roulades, brush with melted butter and steam for approx. 10 minutes.

4 Gently sauté the shallots and diced mango in half the butter. Sprinkle with curry powder, then pour in the Noilly Prat and wine. Simmer until the liquid is reduced by half, then stir in the fish stock and, once again, reduce to half the quantity. Add the cream and reduce.

5 Purée the sauce and mix with the remaining butter. Season to taste with salt, pepper and lime juice. Sauté the 4 reserved langoustines for 1–2 minutes in olive oil. Arrange the roulades on a layer of sauce and garnish with the sautéed langoustines.

Barbecued
squid

Serves 4

600 g squid, ready to cook

1 bunch parsley

4 garlic cloves

2 tbsp olive oil

1 tbsp lemon juice

salt

black pepper

Preparation time: approx.
15 minutes (plus cooking time)
Per portion approx. 184 kcal/
773 kJ
24 g P, 7 g F, 5 g CH

1 Wash and dry the squid, then cut into pieces. Wash the parsley, shake dry and chop finely. Peel and finely chop the garlic. Mix with the parsley and set aside.

2 Heat a barbecue grill, line the grill with aluminium foil and brush with a little olive oil. Place the squid on the grill and cook for about 5 minutes until they turn pink.

3 Turn occasionally and brush with the remaining oil. Once they are lightly browned, they are ready to serve.

4 Drizzle the squid with lemon juice and season generously with salt and pepper. Sprinkle with the parsley-and-garlic mixture and serve. Grilled potatoes make an excellent accompaniment to this dish.

Tip

Frozen squid may also be used for this recipe in which case you should defrost the squid before use and allow twice the amount of cooking time.

Herring salad
with bacon and onions

Serves 4

2 salted herrings, ready to cook

1 kg potatoes, cooked in their skins

2 small tart apples

4 gherkins

approx. 125 ml vegetable stock

4 tbsp wine vinegar

salt

pepper

sugar

125 g streaky bacon

1 onion

Preparation time: approx. 25 minutes (plus soaking and steeping time)
Per portion approx. 355 kcal/ 1491 kJ
25 g P, 7 g F, 46 g CH

1 Leave the herrings to soak overnight in cold water. Peel and slice the potatoes.

2 Drain the herrings, remove the heads and backbone. Wash and drain the filleted fish, then pat dry.

3 Peel and core the apples. Cut the herring fillets, apples and gherkins into fine strips and combine with the potatoes.

4 Pour the hot vegetable stock over the potatoes and leave all the ingredients to cool. Mix the wine vinegar, salt, pepper and sugar into a spicy dressing, and pour over the salad. Gently mix the salad ingredients together, then cover and chill for 60 minutes in the refrigerator.

5 Before serving, chop the bacon into small pieces, peel and finely chop the onion. Heat the bacon in a frying pan until the fat begins to run, then cook the onions in the juices. Sprinkle the bacon and onions over the herring salad whilst still hot.

Soups & stews

Spicy pollock

and coconut soup

Serves 4

2 onions
1 garlic clove
2 green peppers
2 carrots
4 tbsp oil
1–2 tbsp curry powder
75 g shredded coconut
pinch of cayenne pepper
125 ml fish or vegetable stock
salt
1–2 tsp honey
1 bunch flat-leaf parsley
500 g pollock fillet
2 tbsp shredded coconut, toasted

Preparation time: approx.
30 minutes (plus cooking time)
Per portion approx. 343 kcal/
1439 kJ
17 g P, 26 g F, 12 g CH

1 Peel and finely chop the onions and garlic. Clean and wash the green peppers, then cut in half, remove the stalks and seeds and finely chop. Peel and finely chop the carrots.

2 Heat the oil in a saucepan and gently fry the onions along with the garlic and vegetables. Sprinkle curry powder over all the ingredients and continue cooking gently for another minute. Add the shredded coconut and cayenne pepper, and cook for 1 minute.

3 Pour in 900 ml water and the fish stock and season to taste with salt and honey. Cover the saucepan with a lid and simmer the soup for approx. 15 minutes over a moderate heat.

4 Wash the parsley, shake it dry and finely chop. Wash the fish, pat dry and cut into bite-sized pieces. Purée the soup, then strain it back into the saucepan through a fine sieve.

5 Bring the soup to a boil, add the chunks of fish and cook for approx. 5 minutes until tender. Season the soup to taste again and stir in the parsley. Serve the soup garnished with the toasted coconut flakes.

Turbot carpaccio
in stock

Serves 4

approx. 300 g turbot
carcasses
1 bunch soup greens
½ leek
100 g celery
100 g beetroot
300 g fresh turbot fillet
½ packet saffron strands
salt
pepper

Preparation time: approx.
20 minutes (plus cooking time)
Per portion approx. 100 kcal/
414 kJ
15 g P, 2 g F, 6 g CH

1 Place the fish carcasses in a saucepan. Clean, wash and, if necessary, peel the soup greens, then roughly chop them into small pieces before adding to the saucepan. Pour in 750 ml water and bring to a boil. Simmer all the ingredients for about 40 minutes until they form a hearty stock. Strain and continue cooking until the liquid is reduced to about 400 ml.

2 Meanwhile, clean and wash the rest of the vegetables. Slice the leek into thin rings, peel and thinly slice the celery and beetroot.

3 Blanch the individual vegetables in boiling, salted water for approx. 1 minute, plunge in cold water, then drain.

4 Using a very sharp knife, slice the turbot fillet into wafer-thin slices and divide between 4 soup bowls, then place the blanched vegetables in the centre.

5 Stir the saffron strands into the hot turbot soup, season with salt and pepper. Pour the soup into the prepared soup bowls and serve.

Mixed seafood
in ginger stock

Serves 4

6 tbsp fish sauce
2 large pieces of ginger
1 bunch coriander
1 courgette
1 large leek
1 carrot
1 kaffir lime
100 g shiitake mushrooms
200 g king prawns
12 scampi
4 swimmer crabs
400 g white fish meat
chilli oil

Preparation time: approx.
25 minutes (plus cooking time)
Per portion approx. 310 kcal/
1299 kJ
46 g P, 7 g F, 12 g CH

1 Bring 3 l water to a boil with the fish sauce and unpeeled, diced ginger and simmer for 10 minutes. Strain the mixture through a sieve. Wash the coriander, shake it dry, then pull off the leaves.

2 Wash and dry the courgette, leek and carrot, then clean or peel the vegetables and cut into slices. Cut the lime in half. Clean the shiitake mushrooms and slice thinly.

3 Wash the prawns, scampi, swimmer crabs and fish meat, dab with paper towel to dry thoroughly.

4 Place all the seafood, fish and vegetables in a wok, pour in the ginger stock and bring to a boil. Simmer gently for 5 minutes. Sprinkle with coriander leaves and drizzle with a little chilli oil.

Swimmer crabs
with curry sauce and coriander

Serves 4

12 swimmer crabs
4 tbsp vegetable oil
1 tbsp yellow curry paste
1 tbsp palm sugar
4 tbsp oyster sauce
2 tbsp fish sauce
2 tins coconut milk
(400 ml each)
5 coriander leaves
1 tbsp shredded coconut

Preparation time: approx.
20 minutes
Per portion approx. 232 kcal/
970 kJ
17 g P, 15 g F, 7 g CH

1 Wash the swimmer crabs thoroughly in running water, dry well and cut in half.

2 Heat the oil in a wok and quickly sear the crabs. Then, add the curry paste, the finely chopped palm sugar, oyster sauce and fish sauce, and fry lightly.

3 Pour in the coconut milk, then simmer until the crabs have turned completely red.

4 Shred the coriander leaves into thin strips, add to the sauce and sprinkle with shredded coconut before serving.

Creamy mussel soup
with smoked bacon

Serves 4

1.25 kg common mussels
1 bunch soup greens
1 garlic clove
1 tbsp oil
750 ml dry white wine
100 g smoked bacon
2 onions
3 potatoes
1 tbsp flour
250 ml milk
salt
pepper
250 ml cream

Preparation time approx.
45 minutes (plus cooking time)
Per portion approx. 540 kcal/
2268 kJ
41 g P, 29 g F, 26 g CH

1 Clean the mussels thoroughly and pull off the beards, discarding any that have remained open. Clean and finely chop the soup greens. Peel and coarsely chop the garlic clove.

2 Heat the oil in a saucepan and gently fry the garlic and vegetables. Pour in the wine and add the mussels. Cook for about 15 minutes.

3 Remove the mussels from the saucepan, retaining the stock. Holding the mussels over the pan, scoop the flesh from their shells. Discard any that are still shut after cooking.

4 Dice the bacon and sweat out the fat in a frying pan. Next, remove the diced bacon from the pan. Peel and dice the onions, then fry gently in the bacon fat.

5 Peel and dice the potatoes. Sprinkle the onions with flour. Add the potatoes, milk and mussel stock, then season with salt and pepper. Cover and simmer for about 10 minutes.

6 Finally, stir in the cream, bacon and mussels and simmer for another 3 minutes.

Sweet-and-sour fish soup
with glass noodles

Serves 4

50 g glass noodles

150 g fish fillet (e.g. redfish or pollock)

8 large prawns

1 tbsp lemon juice

1 tomato

200 g pak choi (Chinese white mustard cabbage)

1 bunch spring onions

1 celery stick

750 ml chicken stock

1 tbsp red wine vinegar

1 tbsp brown sugar

1 tbsp soy sauce

salt

small amount coriander or flat-leaf parsley to garnish

Preparation time: approx.
15 minutes (plus cooking time)
Per portion approx. 350 kcal/
1470 kJ
57 g P, 7 g F, 13 g CH

1 Place the glass noodles in a bowl, cover with warm water and leave to soak for approx. 10 minutes. Drain through a sieve and cut them into shorter lengths.

2 Dice the fish fillet. Break open the shells, remove the prawns and de-vein. Wash and dry the prawns with paper towel. Sprinkle the fish and prawns with lemon juice, and leave to marinate for a little while.

3 Meanwhile, cut a cross in the tomato skin, plunge in boiling water, then peel off the skin. Cut out the stalk and remove the seeds, then finely dice.

4 Wash the pak choi, pat dry and tear it into bite-sized pieces. Clean and wash the spring onions, then cut into thin rings. Clean and wash the celery, then cut it into small pieces.

5 Bring the stock to a boil, season with vinegar, sugar and soy sauce. Simmer the vegetables in the stock for approx. 2 minutes. Add the fish and prawns and cook for approx. 1 minute. Stir in the glass noodles and season the soup with salt. Serve sprinkled with a garnish of coriander or parsley.

Rich crab soup
with sherry

Serves 4

1 large cooked crab
3 tbsp butter
1 onion
2 tbsp flour
1.15 l milk
90 ml sherry
salt, pepper, nutmeg
150 ml cream
½ bunch freshly chopped
chives

Preparation time: approx.
30 minutes (plus frying and
cooking time)
Per portion approx. 338 kcal/
1418 kJ
6 g P, 17 g F, 6 g CH

1 Remove the meat from the crab. Cut off the legs and large pincers, break them open and scoop out the meat.

2 Turn the crab shell over, then press out and discard the innards, as well as the underbelly. Scoop out the white meat. Scrape out the brown crab meat and set both aside for later.

3 Heat the butter in a saucepan. Peel and finely dice the onion, fry in the butter until it turns translucent. Sprinkle with flour, then pour in the milk and sherry. Stir all the ingredients together and simmer gently until the mixture turns creamy.

4 Add the brown crab meat to the soup and simmer for 20 minutes. Season with salt, pepper and nutmeg. Add the white meat (including the meat from the claws) and simmer for a further 5 minutes.

5 Pour the crab soup into bowls. Whisk the cream until stiff and add a blob of cream to each bowl. Garnish with chopped chives and serve with toasted wholemeal bread.

French
bouillabaisse

Serves 4

1 kg mixed Mediterranean fish, ready to cook (e.g. scorpion fish, John Dory, gurnard, monkfish or sea bass)

1 onion

4 potatoes

4 beef tomatoes

½ fennel root

1 bunch parsley

4 tbsp olive oil

4 bay leaves

herbes de Provence

salt

freshly ground pepper

4 packets saffron

5 garlic cloves

500 ml dry white wine

1 dried chilli pepper

1 slice white bread, crust removed

30 ml cold-pressed olive oil

8 slices baguette

Preparation time: approx. 25 minutes (plus cooking time)
Per portion approx. 483 kcal/ 2027 kJ
42 g P, 19 g F, 23 g CH

1 Cut the fish into portion-sized pieces. Peel and dice the onion. Peel and wash the potatoes, then grate into thin slices. Dice the tomatoes. Clean, wash and slice the fennel root. Chop the parsley.

2 Sweat the onion in oil. Briefly fry the vegetables with the onion. Add the bay leaves, parsley, herbes de Provence, salt, pepper and saffron. Peel the garlic and crush 4 cloves, then add to the frying pan and cook for approx. 10 minutes.

3 Mix the wine with 500 ml water and bring to a boil. Add the fish to the vegetables and cook together for approx. 3 minutes. Pour in the bubbling wine mixture, remove the pan from the heat and leave to steep for approx. 15–20 minutes.

4 Crush 1 garlic clove with the dried chilli. Soak the bread in water, then squeeze out the water and purée with the garlic and chilli, adding the oil to the mixer in a thin stream. Toast the baguette and spread each slice with the purée, place 2 slices in each soup bowl and fill with soup.

Creamy fish soup
with tomatoes

Serves 4

400 g white fish fillet

1 onion

2 garlic cloves

4 potatoes

3 tbsp butter

400 g tomatoes, tinned

½ bunch freshly chopped parsley

2 bay leaves

salt

pepper

pinch of cayenne pepper

500 ml fish stock

100 ml cream

dill to garnish

Preparation time: approx.
20 minutes (plus cooking time)
Per portion approx. 209 kcal/
878 kJ
19 g P, 13 g F, 5 g CH

1 Cut the fish fillets into small pieces. Peel and finely dice the onions and garlic. Peel and thinly slice the potatoes.

2 Heat the butter in a saucepan and sweat the onions and garlic. Add the potato slices and sauté briefly. Pour in 100 ml water and simmer all the ingredients for about 10 minutes.

3 Add the tomatoes, parsley and spices, then the fish chunks. Pour in the fish stock and simmer all the ingredients for a further 8 minutes.

4 Stir the cream into the soup, season to taste with salt and pepper. Remove and discard the bay leaves, garnish the soup with a sprinkle of dill. Serve with toasted bread.

Tuna goulash
with paprika

Serves 4

500 g tuna fillet

1 lemon

salt

freshly ground pepper

2 onions

3 garlic cloves

1 green pepper

1 red pepper

1 chilli pepper

500 g beef tomatoes

2 tbsp olive oil

2 tsp mild paprika powder

500 g potatoes

250 ml dry white wine

Preparation time: approx.
20 minutes (plus marinating and
cooking time)
Per portion approx. 485 kcal/
2037 kJ
33 g P, 22 g F, 30 g CH

1 Rinse the tuna, pat dry, then cut into bite-sized pieces. Squeeze the juice from the lemon. Drizzle lemon juice over the chunks of tuna fish, season with salt and pepper and marinate for 30 minutes.

2 Peel and finely dice the onions and garlic. Clean and wash the peppers and chilli, cut in half, remove the stalks and seeds, then cut into strips. Reserve a little paprika powder for the garnish. Make a cross-shaped incision in the tomatoes, plunge them in boiling water and peel off the skins. Cut out the stalks, remove the seeds, then dice.

3 Heat the oil in a frying pan and fry the onions until translucent. Add the garlic and peppers, then cook over a low heat for approx. 5 minutes. Sprinkle the ingredients with paprika powder.

4 Add the tomatoes, chilli, salt and pepper to the ingredients in the frying pan and simmer uncovered for 10 minutes. Peel the potatoes, wash, dice, then add to the mixture along with the wine. Cover and cook for approx. 10 minutes.

5 Finally, stir in the tuna chunks and leave to cook in the mixture for approx. 5 minutes. Season the goulash to taste and serve garnished with a few strips of bell pepper.

Light fish dishes

Zander curry
with water chestnuts

Serves 4

800 g zander fillet

3 tbsp fish sauce

120 g aubergine

1 tbsp red curry paste

1 tin coconut milk (400 ml)

100 ml water

1 tbsp palm sugar

200 g water chestnuts

2 kaffir lime leaves

Preparation time: approx.
30 minutes (plus 10 minutes to
marinate)
Per portion approx. 315 kcal/
1320 kJ
47 g P, 3 g F , 25 g CH

1 Wash the zander fillet, pat dry and cut into bite-sized portions. Marinate the fish for 10 minutes in 2 tablespoons of fish sauce. Wash and dry the aubergine, then cut into pieces.

2 Mix the curry paste with 200 ml coconut milk, water and grated palm sugar. Bring to a boil, stirring constantly. Add the remaining coconut milk, then add the diced aubergine and simmer gently for about 10 minutes. Flavour with fish sauce.

3 Thoroughly drain the chestnuts, then add to the mixture. Add the fish pieces and simmer for a few minutes until cooked.

4 Slice the lime leaves into fine strips, add to the mixture, then serve in small bowls.

Fried perch
with red curry and lychees

Serves 4

500 g perch fillet, skinned
4 tbsp fish sauce
1 bitter cucumber
1 fresh, large chilli pepper
4 tbsp vegetable oil
1 tbsp palm sugar
1 tbsp red curry paste
2 tins unsweetened coconut
milk (400 ml each)
1 tin lychees (400 g)

Preparation time: approx.
15 minutes
Per portion approx. 318 kcal/
1332 kJ
25 g P, 13 g F, 24 g CH

1 Wash the perch fillet, pat dry and cut into 3-cm squares.

2 Cut the bitter cucumber in half, de-seed and cut into ½-cm thick slices. Slice the chilli pepper into thin rings.

3 Heat the oil in a wok, add the finely chopped palm sugar and curry paste. Add the coconut milk and bring to a boil. Add the bitter cucumber and simmer gently for 5 minutes.

4 Drain the lychees and add to the other ingredients. Add the fish chunks to the mixture and marinate for another 2 minutes. Sprinkle all the ingredients with chilli rings.

Trout au bleu

Serves 4

1 small onion

1 carrot

1 unwaxed lemon

2 bay leaves

125 ml dry white wine

4 trout, ready to cook
(approx. 250 g each)

1 tbsp salt

¼ bunch parsley

Preparation time: approx.
20 minutes (plus cooking time)
Per portion approx. 345 kcal/
1449 kJ
58 g P, 7 g F, 5 g CH

1 In a saucepan, bring 2 l water to a boil.

2 Wipe the onion clean, but do not peel. Peel and finely slice the carrot. Wash the lemon, then cut half of it into slices.

3 Add the onion and carrot to the boiling water. Add the bay leaves, sliced lemon and wine to the saucepan, and simmer the stock for 30 minutes.

4 Rinse the trout in running water, then pat dry, taking care not to damage the skin. Add salt to the broth, then add the trout to the liquid. Bring the stock back to a boil and cook the trout over a low heat for approx. 20 minutes until tender. The trout are cooked when the dorsal fin pulls away easily.

5 Remove the trout from the fish stock and arrange on a platter. Wash, dry and finely chop the parsley. Garnish the trout with parsley and the remaining lemon.

Trout meunière

Serves 4

4 trout, ready to cook
(250–350 g each)
4 tbsp lemon juice
salt
50 g flour
80 g butter
¼ bunch parsley

Preparation time: approx.
15 minutes (plus resting and
cooking time)
Per portion approx. 553 kcal/
2321 kJ
63 g P, 29 g F, 13 g CH

1 Rinse the trout under running water, then pat dry.

2 Drizzle 3 tablespoons of lemon juice over the trout inside and outside. Set aside for 15 minutes. Rub salt on the trout on the inside and outside, and carefully toss in flour.

3 Heat approx. ⅔ of the butter in a frying pan and carefully fry the trout on both sides for approx. 10 minutes until golden brown. The trout are cooked when the dorsal fin pulls away easily.

4 Wash, dry and finely chop the parsley.

5 Remove the trout from the frying pan and arrange on a warm platter.

6 Heat the remaining butter and the remaining lemon juice in the fat left in the frying pan. Spoon this over the trout and sprinkle with parsley. Serve with baby parsley potatoes and green salad.

Red snapper
wrapped in banana leaf

Serves 4

2 sprigs lime leaves

2 sprigs Thai basil

75 ml coconut cream

1–2 tsp red curry paste

1–2 tsp fish sauce

1 tsp brown sugar

1 banana leaf (Asian food store)

1 pinch red or green chilli paste in oil

500 g red snapper fillet

Preparation time: approx. 15 minutes (plus baking time)
Per portion approx. 143 kcal/600 kJ
24 g P, 5 g F, 2 g CH

1 Pre-heat the oven to 180 °C (Gas Mark 4). Wash the lime and basil leaves and shake dry, then tear the leaves off the stems. Slice the lime and basil leaves into thin strips and set aside.

2 To make the marinade, place the coconut cream in a mixing bowl with 1–2 teaspoons of curry paste (depending on how hot it is), fish sauce and sugar, stirring vigorously until the sugar has completely dissolved.

3 Cut the banana leaf in half lengthwise, removing the middle vein and divide into 4 equal-sized pieces (approx. 30 x 35 cm). Gently warm the banana leaves in a dry frying-pan until the surface develops a waxy appearance.

4 Spread a little chilli paste over the banana leaves. Rinse the fish, then pat dry and cut into 4 portions. Brush the fish segments with marinade.

5 Place a piece of fish on each portion of banana leaf, then top each one with basil and lime leaves. Wrap each piece of fish firmly in a banana leaf parcel and bake in the pre-heated oven for approx. 20 minutes. Serve wrapped in the leaf with a side dish of rice.

Fried scallops
with spring onions

Serves 4

12 scallops, removed from
their shells and without roe
pinch of lemon zest
1 tbsp toasted sesame oil
1 bunch spring onions
200 g tomatoes
1 garlic clove
1 red chilli pepper
4 tbsp sunflower oil
1 tsp freshly grated ginger
2 tbsp oyster sauce
2 tbsp fish sauce

Preparation time: approx.
35 minutes (plus 10 minutes
marinating time)
Per portion approx. 142 kcal/
593 kJ
12 g P, 8 g F, 4 g CH

1 Wash the scallops thoroughly in running water, dry well and marinate in lemon zest and sesame oil for 10 minutes.

2 Wash the spring onions and cut diagonally into 4-cm lengths. Make incisions in the tomato skins, plunge them briefly in boiling water, then rinse in cold water, before peeling off the skins. Cut into quarters, remove the seeds and slice into strips. Finely chop the peeled garlic and de-seeded chilli pepper.

3 Using half the oil, fry the spring onions in the wok. Add the tomatoes, ginger, garlic and chilli and cook for a further 3 minutes. Season to taste with oyster and fish sauce. Remove the ingredients from the wok.

4 Heat the remaining oil in the wok and fry the scallops until golden brown. Arrange on plates with the spring onion and tomato mixture.

Sweet-and-sour sea bream

with leek and carrot strips

Serves 4

4 sea bream fillets,
unskinned (120 g each)
6 medium-sized carrots
4 leeks
4 tbsp vegetable oil
2 tbsp tomato ketchup
4 tbsp sweet-and-sour sauce
2 tbsp fish sauce
2 sprigs coriander

Preparation time: approx.
25 minutes
Per portion approx. 347 kcal/
1455 kJ
31 g P, 16 g F, 15 g CH

1 Wash the fish fillets, pat dry and remove any bones. Cut into 3-cm segments. Wash and peel the carrots, then, using a vegetable peeler, shave into strips. Cut the leeks into thin strips approx. 15 cm in length. Wash and shake dry.

2 Heat 2 tablespoons of oil in a wok and briefly fry the fish pieces on the skin side only, then remove from the wok.

3 Using the rest of the oil, fry the vegetables over a high heat until softened, then season with sweet-and-sour sauce and add the fish sauce.

4 Return the fish segments to the wok and carefully mix with the other ingredients. Finally, stir in the finely chopped coriander. Add a little additional water to the sauce, if necessary, to prevent it becoming too dry.

Bream

on a bed of mixed vegetables

Serves 4

1.2 kg bream, ready to cook

3 tbsp lemon juice

salt

pepper

4–6 garlic cloves

1 unwaxed lemon

1 yellow, 1 red and 1 green
pepper

2 very small courgettes

600 g beef tomatoes

1 bunch parsley

2 sprigs rosemary

175 ml dry white wine

4–5 tbsp olive oil

Preparation time: approx.
25 minutes (plus cooking time)
Per portion approx. 493 kcal/
2068 kJ
66 g P, 15 g F, 15 g CH

1 Pre-heat the oven to 200 °C (Gas Mark 6). Sprinkle the fish inside and out with lemon juice, then season with salt and pepper. Peel the garlic, then slice 3 of the garlic cloves in half lengthwise. Rinse the lemon in hot water, dry and cut into 6 segments.

2 Using a sharp knife, make 3 slits on either side of the fish. Insert half a garlic clove and a lemon segment into each slit.

3 Clean and wash the bell peppers, cut in half and slice into thin strips. Wash and thinly slice the courgettes. Cut a cross-shaped incision in each tomato skin, plunge in boiling water, then peel off the skins. Cut in half, remove the stalks and roughly chop.

4 Wash the parsley and rosemary, shake dry and finely chop the leaves. Mix the herbs with the vegetables, then crush and add the remaining garlic. Season with salt and pepper, then tip all the ingredients into a large baking dish and pour in the wine.

5 Lay the fish on the bed of vegetables and drizzle the olive oil over the top. Cover and bake in the oven for approx. 15 minutes. Remove the cover from the dish, then reduce the heat to approx. 180 °C (Gas Mark 4) and continue to bake for approx. 25 minutes. Serve in the baking dish.

Clam chowder

Serves 4

1.5 kg cockles or clams

4 onions, 4 carrots,
4 parsnips, 4 celery sticks

250 ml dry white wine

250 ml vegetable stock

2 bay leaves

½ tbsp each allspice berries
and peppercorns

2–3 tbsp lemon zest

2 tbsp each celery and
fennel seeds

salt

pepper

3–4 sprigs thyme

Preparation time: approx.
30 minutes (plus cooking time)
Per portion approx. 545 kcal/
2289 kJ
52 g P, 8 g F, 51 g CH

1 Pre-heat the oven to 200 °C (Gas Mark 6). Wash the shellfish and discard any which remain partially open. Peel and dice the onions. Clean, wash, peel and dice the carrots, parsnips and celery.

2 Soak a clay pot before use, then add the clams or cockles, followed by the vegetables. Pour in the white wine and vegetable stock. Add the bay leaves, allspice and peppercorns, then season all the ingredients with lemon zest, celery and fennel seeds, salt and pepper. Wash and drain the sprigs of thyme and add to the clay pot.

3 Place the lid on the pot and cook in the oven for 30–35 minutes. At the end of this time, remove the sprigs of thyme and discard any clams which are still closed.

4 Serve the clam chowder with crispy baguette or rice.

Corsican-style mussels

Serves 4

2 kg mussels
2 small onions
300 ml dry white wine
300 ml water
1 bay leaf
1 leek
½ small fennel bulb
1 carrot
125 g celeriac
40 g butter
1 tbsp cornstarch
100 g low-fat crème fraîche
salt
1 tsp rose paprika

Preparation time: approx.
25 minutes (plus cooking time)
Per portion approx. 540 kcal/
2268 kJ
53 g P, 23 g F, 26 g CH

1 Brush the mussels vigorously under running cold water and remove the beards. Discard any mussels which are not fully closed.

2 To make the stock, peel and dice the onions and place them in a large saucepan with the wine, water and the bay leaf, and bring to a boil.

3 Add the mussels and leave to simmer for approx. 5 minutes over a very low heat, giving the pan a vigorous shake from time to time. Remove the mussels from the saucepan and keep warm. Reserve the cooking water.

4 Clean or peel the vegetables, wash and cut into very thin strips. Melt the butter in the saucepan, add the vegetables, stirring all the time, and sweat for approx. 5 minutes. Pour in the reserved mussel stock and thicken by adding a little cornstarch. Remove from the heat and stir in the crème fraîche. Season generously with salt and paprika.

5 Scoop the mussels from their shells, discarding any which have not opened during cooking. Divide the mussels into portions, top with hot vegetable sauce and serve immediately.

Cod
with mustard-and-herb sauce

Serves 4

½ bunch spring onions

200 ml dry white wine

5 white peppercorns

1½ tsp salt

4 cod fillets (approx. 600 g)

1 tbsp sugar

2 tbsp malt vinegar

2 tbsp mild mustard

½ bunch freshly chopped herbs (e.g. dill, chives, chervil, parsley)

7 tbsp sunflower oil

salt

pepper

Preparation time: approx. 20 minutes (plus cooking time)
Per portion approx. 145 kcal/ 607 kJ
26 g P, 4 g F, 2 g CH

1 Clean and finely chop the spring onions. Pour the white wine and 300 ml water into a saucepan with the spring onions, peppercorns and salt. Bring to a boil and simmer for about 10 minutes.

2 Place the fish fillets in a saucepan. Filter the wine mixture through a sieve and pour over the cod fillets. Simmer over a low heat for about 8 minutes.

3 In a bowl, combine the sugar, vinegar, mustard and herbs. Add the oil, a few drops at a time, and mix thoroughly. Season with salt and pepper.

4 Serve the fish fillets with the mustard and herb sauce.

Poached cod
with horseradish

Serves 4

½ bunch spring onions
200 ml dry white wine
5 white peppercorns
1½ tsp salt
4 cod fillets (approx. 600 g)
4 eggs
½ bunch parsley
4 tsp freshly grated
horseradish

Preparation time: approx.
20 minutes (plus cooking time)
Per portion approx. 240 kcal/
1011 kJ
34 g P, 8 g F, 3 g CH

1 Clean and finely chop the spring onions. Pour the white wine into a saucepan along with 300 ml water, the spring onions, peppercorns and salt. Bring to a boil and simmer for approx. 10 minutes.

2 Place the fish fillets in a saucepan. Filter the wine mixture through a sieve and pour over the cod. Simmer for approx. 8 minutes over a gentle heat.

3 Boil the eggs for about 10 minutes until hard. Plunge in cold water, leave to cool, then peel and dice. Finely chop the parsley.

4 Serve the fish fillets with boiled potatoes, parsley, diced egg and horseradish. Accompany the dish with melted butter, if desired.

Asian-style stuffed squid

Serves 4

750 g small squid, ready to cook, with the head attached
60 g Chinese cabbage
60 g soy bean sprouts
3 spring onions
2 garlic cloves
2 tbsp vegetable oil
2 shiitake mushrooms
1½ tbsp light soy sauce
4 tsp sesame oil
salt
pepper
100 g lean minced beef

Preparation time: 30 minutes
(plus cooking and steaming time)
Per portion approx. 258 kcal/
1082 kJ
37 g P, 9 g F, 7 g CH

1 Wash the squid. Cut off the head and tentacles, then separate the tentacles from the head. Discard the head and chop the tentacles into small pieces. Wash the Chinese cabbage and cut into strips. Wash and drain the soy bean sprouts. Clean and wash the spring onions, then slice into rings. Peel and finely chop the garlic.

2 Heat the oil in a frying pan, then sauté the diced squid tentacles with the vegetables and garlic for a few minutes. Clean, wash and roughly chop the mushrooms, then add to the vegetable mixture. Cook for 1 minute, then add the soy sauce and 2 teaspoons of sesame oil to the mixture. Season to taste with salt and pepper.

3 Stuff the squid with the mixture in the frying pan and the minced beef, then close the openings. Place the squid in a bowl, then drizzle with the remaining sesame oil. Using a steamer, cook over boiling water for approx. 20 minutes. Remove the squid from the steamer and cut into slices. Serve with soy sauce or a selection of dips.

Fish stew
with herbs

Serves 4

400 g potatoes
1 leek
1 onion
4 tbsp butter
salt
pepper
nutmeg
1 tsp mustard
juice and grated zest of
½ unwaxed lemon
500 ml fish stock
125 ml cream
500 g cod fillets
1 egg yolk
2 tbsp freshly chopped herbs
(chives, parsley, dill, chervil)

Preparation time: approx.
30 minutes (plus cooking time)
Per portion approx. 303 kcal/
1271 kJ
28 g P, 13 g F, 18 g CH

1 Peel and finely dice the potatoes. Clean the leek, remove the tough, dark green leaves, then thoroughly wash the rest of the leek and slice into rings. Peel and dice the onion.

2 Melt the butter in a saucepan and fry the diced onion until translucent. Add the potatoes and leek, and fry gently. Season with salt, pepper, nutmeg, mustard and lemon zest.

3 Pour in the fish stock and stir in 100 ml cream. Bring the ingredients to a boil and cook over a low heat for 15–20 minutes.

4 Wash the fish fillet, pat dry and cut into chunks. Sprinkle with lemon juice and rub in salt and pepper.

5 Stir the pieces of fish into the vegetable mixture and cook in the steam for a further 10 minutes.

6 Lightly beat the egg yolk with the remaining cream, then stir into the stew without actually cooking the mixture any further. Serve the stew sprinkled with herbs.

Carp goulash
with peppers and sour cream

Serves 4

1.2 kg carp, ready to cook

juice of 1 lemon

2 red peppers

salt

white pepper

3 bay leaves

4 allspice berries

1 dried pepperoni chilli

2 onions

2 garlic cloves

approx. 850 g tomatoes (tinned)

100 ml oil

250 ml dry white wine

approx. 850 g preserved peppers (from a jar)

3 tbsp sour cream

mild paprika powder

Preparation time: approx. 35 minutes (plus marinating and cooking time)
Per portion approx. 505 kcal/ 2121 kJ
58 g P, 23 g F, 11 g CH

1. Fillet the carp: make cuts about 3 cm deep on both sides from the head to the tail down the backbone and down the sides and remove the fish fillets. Divide into bite-sized pieces, drizzle with lemon juice and leave to marinate for approx. 20 minutes.

2. Clean and wash the red peppers, then cut in half. Remove the stalks and seeds, then cut the peppers into strips. Bring 1 l water to a boil, then add the peppers, along with the salt, pepper, bay leaves, allspice berries, pepperoni chilli and fish chunks. Skim off any foam and simmer for approx. 45 minutes.

3. Peel and finely dice the onions and garlic. Chop the tinned tomatoes into smaller pieces. In a frying pan, heat the oil, then fry the onions and garlic until translucent. Pour in the wine. Drain the preserved peppers, then add to the onion mixture along with the tomatoes in their juice. Cover and simmer for approx. 35 minutes.

4. Stir in the sour cream and cook for another 3 minutes. Press all the ingredients through a sieve and return to a saucepan, add a little fish stock and season generously with salt, pepper and paprika powder. Add the fish segments and leave in the soup for 7–8 minutes until tender. Do not cook further or the fish will fall apart. Rice makes an excellent accompaniment to this dish.

Fish cakes
with herbs

Serves 4

250 g potatoes
salt
150 g fresh fish fillet
pepper
150 g smoked fish fillet
2 tbsp chopped parsley
3 tbsp chopped dill
3 tbsp mayonnaise
hot pepper sauce
breadcrumbs for coating
80 g butter
2 tbsp crème fraîche
2 tsp chopped capers
juice of ¼ lemon
pinch of sugar

Preparation time: approx.
25 minutes (plus baking time)
Per portion approx. 252 kcal/
1061 kJ
18 g P, 12 g F, 18 g CH

1 Pre-heat the oven to 200 °C (Gas Mark 6). Peel, wash and roughly dice the potatoes, then cook in salted water and drain.

2 Season the fish with salt and pepper, and wrap tightly in buttered aluminium foil. Cook in the pre-heated oven for approx. 12–15 minutes. Open the parcel, pour the cooking juices onto the cooked potatoes and mash thoroughly.

3 Skin and fillet the smoked fish, then mix with the potatoes. Finely chop the cooked fish and add to the potato mixture. Add half the herbs and 1 tablespoon of mayonnaise. Season with hot pepper sauce, salt and pepper. Shape the mixture into 8 little patties, toss in breadcrumbs and press down gently to flatten slightly.

4 Line a baking sheet with baking paper and grease with 1 tablespoon of butter. Melt the remaining butter, then brush the fish cakes and arrange on the baking sheet. Increase the oven heat to 220 °C (Gas Mark 7) and bake for approx. 20 minutes until crisp and golden brown.

5 Mix the remaining herbs with the crème fraîche and rest of the mayonnaise. Drain the capers and stir into the sauce. Season with salt, pepper, lemon juice and sugar. Serve the fish cakes with an accompaniment of herb sauce.

Pan-fried dishes

Paella marinara

Serves 4

4 garlic cloves
juice of ½ lemon
3 tbsp olive oil
500 g fresh redfish fillet
250 g mixed seafood or
prawns (frozen)
1 large onion
1 large red chilli pepper
250 g long grain rice
approx. 500 ml vegetable
stock
3 saffron strands
100 g peas (frozen)
3 lemon slices

Preparation time: approx.
20 minutes (plus chilling and
cooking time)
Per portion approx. 580 kcal/
2436 kJ
42 g P, 22 g F, 53 g CH

1 Peel the garlic. Mix the lemon juice with 2 table-spoons of oil, add 2 crushed garlic cloves. Wash the fish and pat dry, then add to lemon juice and garlic, and refrigerate for approx. 30 minutes.

2 Meanwhile, defrost the mixed seafood or prawns and drain off any excess water. Peel and dice the onion. Chop the remaining garlic cloves. Cut the chilli pepper in half, remove the seeds and cut into strips.

3 Using a special paella pan or a large frying pan, heat the rest of the oil and fry the onions, garlic and chilli pepper for approx. 5 minutes.

4 Add the rice, cook, stirring constantly, until translucent, then pour in the vegetable stock. Add the saffron, cover and cook for about 10 minutes over a low heat.

5 Remove the fish from the marinade, place it on top of the rice and cook for approx. 5 minutes. Add the seafood mixture or prawns and peas, and cook with the other ingredients for 4 minutes. Garnish the paella with the lemon slices and serve in the pan.

Sweet-and-sour carp

Serves 4

1 carp, ready to cook

2 tbsp light soy sauce

1 tbsp rice wine

salt

100 g cornflour

100 ml oil for frying

2 tbsp coconut oil

2 chopped red chilli peppers

2 crushed garlic cloves

1 tsp freshly grated ginger

2 tbsp vinegar

1½ tsp sugar

½ tsp sesame oil

175 ml fish stock

pepper

3 spring onions, sliced into rings

Preparation time: approx.
20 minutes (plus marinating and
frying time)
Per portion approx. 253 kcal/
1060 kJ
28 g P, 5 g F, 23 g CH

1 Wash the carp, then rub the fish with soy sauce, rice wine and ½ teaspoon of salt. Leave to marinate for approx. 30 minutes.

2 Combine 90 g cornflour with 100 ml water. Make diagonal cuts in the fish on both sides. Dip in the batter.

3 Pour the oil into an electric fish fryer and heat to a high temperature. Place the fish in the fryer and fry for about 10 minutes at a moderate heat, turning once. Remove and drain on paper towel.

4 Heat the coconut oil in a wok, then fry the chilli peppers, garlic and ginger for about 1½ minutes. Blend in the vinegar, sugar and sesame oil. Stir the remaining cornflour into the fish stock and add to the sauce. Once the sauce has thickened slightly, season to taste with salt and pepper. Arrange the fish on a platter and sprinkle with spring onions. Serve the sauce separately.

Plaice

Serves 4

4 plaice, unskinned and
ready to cook
1 cucumber
2 tomatoes
4 shallots
3 tbsp olive oil
salt
pepper
2 tbsp white wine vinegar
3 tbsp butter
small amount of lime juice
1 lime

Preparation time: approx.
35 minutes
Per portion approx. 415 kcal/
1735 kJ
45 g P, 22 g F, 8 g CH

1 Wash the plaice and then pat dry.

2 Wash and peel the cucumber, then cut in half and dice. Wash the tomatoes, remove the stalks, cut in half and finely dice. Peel and finely dice the shallots.

3 Heat 2 tablespoons of oil in a frying pan and fry the shallots until translucent. Add the cucumber and continue to cook until tender. Season generously with salt and pepper, pour in the vinegar and continue to cook until the liquid has nearly evaporated. Stir in the tomatoes and keep the vegetables warm.

4 Heat the butter and remaining oil together in a frying pan, add the plaice and fry for approx. 4 minutes. Turn the fish over and fry for a further 2 minutes. Season with salt and pepper.

5 Arrange the plaice and vegetables on plates, drizzle with a little lime juice and garnish with slices of lime.

Fish in red curry sauce

Serves 4

500 g redfish fillet
1 red pepper
3 spring onions
1 strand lemon grass
1 tbsp peanut oil
2 tbsp red curry paste
400 ml coconut milk
(unsweetened)
4 tbsp oyster sauce
1 tbsp palm sugar
1 tbsp lemon juice
3 tbsp freshly chopped
coriander

Preparation time: approx.
20 minutes (plus cooking time)
Per portion approx. 192 kcal/
807 kJ
21 g P, 9 g F, 8 g CH

1 Cut the fish fillet into strips. Wash the red pepper, cut out the stalk and remove the seeds, then dice. Clean and wash the spring onions, then cut into 3-cm lengths. Remove the outer leaves of the lemon grass and finely chop the lower, white section of stem.

2 Heat the oil in a frying pan and fry the curry paste, stirring constantly. Pour in the coconut milk and oyster sauce, then add the sugar and lemon juice. Add the vegetables along with the lemon grass. Bring the sauce to a boil.

3 Add the fish strips to the bubbling sauce, turn down the heat and cook for about 3 minutes over a low heat. Serve garnished with coriander.

Fish
in batter

Serves 4

800 g mixed fish fillets
(e.g. zander, sturgeon,
redfish, cod)

salt

pepper

2 eggs

125 ml beer

150 g flour

clarified butter for frying

Preparation time: approx.
20 minutes (plus frying time)
Per portion approx. 365 kcal/
1533 kJ
46 g P, 8 g F, 27 g CH

1 Cut the prepared fish into segments about 5 cm in length. Season with salt and pepper.

2 Separate the eggs. Lightly beat the egg yolks with the beer and add the flour. Season with salt. Whisk the egg white until stiff and fold into the beer batter.

3 Heat the clarified butter in a frying pan. Dip the pieces of fish in the batter, allow to drain a little, then fry the fish, one piece at a time, in hot fat until golden brown. Serve with potato salad.

Freshwater whitefish
pan-fried

Serves 4

4 freshwater whitefish, ready
to cook

salt

4 medium-sized onions

½ bunch chervil

100 g flour

100 g butter

½ bunch parsley

Preparation time: approx.
25 minutes
Per portion approx. 535 kcal/
2247 kJ
57 g P, 27 g F, 16 g CH

1 Wash the fish, dab them dry and rub them inside and out with salt. Peel and finely chop the onions. Wash the chervil, shake off any excess water and chop the leaves. Stuff the onions and chervil into the body cavity of each fish.

2 Tip the flour onto a plate and toss the fish in the flour. Heat the butter in a large frying-pan, then fry the fish on all sides for about 20 minutes, turning frequently, until they are well coated with melted butter.

3 Wash the parsley, shake it dry, then chop. Sprinkle the chopped herbs over the cooked fish and serve with potato salad.

Whitefish
with cream sauce

Serves 4

4 ready-to-cook whitefish
salt
4 medium onions
½ bunch chervil
100 g flour
100 g butter
½ bunch dill
½ bunch parsley
750 ml sour cream
pepper

Preparation time: approx.
40 minutes
Per portion approx. 675 kcal/
2835 kJ
26 g P, 49 g F, 33 g CH

1 Wash the whitefish, pat dry and rub inside and out with salt. Peel and finely chop the onions. Wash the chervil, shake dry, then finely chop. Stuff the fish with onions and chervil.

2 Tip the flour onto a plate and toss the fish in it. Heat the butter in a large frying pan, then fry the fish on all sides for about 20 minutes, turning frequently so that they are well coated with butter.

3 Wash the dill and parsley, shake dry and finely chop. Remove the fish from the frying pan and keep warm. Add the sour cream and herbs to the cooking juices in the frying pan and stir well. Season to taste with salt and pepper. Serve the whitefish with the cream sauce and bread.

Catfish with potato
and wild garlic salad

Serves 4

2 tbsp wine vinegar

4 tbsp olive oil

½ tsp mustard

salt

100 ml meat stock

250 g potatoes, cooked in their skins

1 bunch wild garlic

4 catfish fillets, 100 g each

2 eggs

4–6 tbsp breadcrumbs for coating

clarified butter for frying

2 tbsp pumpkin seeds

1–2 tbsp pumpkin seed oil

wild garlic to garnish

Preparation time: approx.
25 minutes (plus marinating time)
Per portion approx. 390 kcal/
1638 kJ
24 g P, 25 g F, 18 g CH

1 To make the marinade, thoroughly blend together the vinegar, oil, mustard and a pinch of salt. Stir in the hot meat stock. Peel the skins off the potatoes whilst still hot, then cut into slices and mix with the marinade.

2 Clean and wash the wild garlic, shake dry, then cut into strips and add to the potato salad. Leave the salad to stand for 1 hour to absorb the flavours.

3 Coat the fish fillets first in lightly beaten egg, then toss them in fine breadcrumbs. Fry them in hot clarified butter until golden brown. Divide the potato salad between 4 plates and garnish with a little wild garlic.

4 Toast the pumpkin seeds in a dry frying pan without fat. Arrange the catfish fillets on the salad, drizzle with a little pumpkin seed oil and sprinkle with pumpkin seeds.

Salmon kebabs
with vegetables

Serves 4

600 g salmon fillet
1 tbsp lemon juice
6 shallots
1 red pepper
½ courgette
200 g fresh king prawns,
peeled
salt
pepper
powdered cardamom and
ginger
5–6 tbsp sesame oil

Preparation time: approx.
30 minutes
Per portion approx. 642 kcal/
2698 kJ
39 g P, 26 g F, 4 g CH

1 Wash and dry the salmon fillet and cut into medium-sized chunks. Drizzle with lemon juice.

2 Peel the shallots and cut in half. Wash the red pepper, cut in half, remove the seeds, then cut into bite-sized pieces. Clean, wash and slice the courgette.

3 Thread the pieces of salmon onto skewers, alternating with chunks of shallot, pepper, courgette and king prawns. Season the kebabs with salt, pepper, cardamom and ginger.

4 Heat the oil in a frying pan and sauté the kebabs on all sides for approx. 6–8 minutes. Remove from the pan, arrange on plates and serve. Tagliatelle in dill sauce makes a perfect accompaniment to this dish.

Plaice roulades
with rocket

Serves 4

750 g plaice fillets
juice of ½ lemon
salt
freshly ground white pepper
1 small shallot
400 g oyster mushrooms
3 tbsp butter
2 tbsp dry sherry
200 g crème fraîche
1 bunch rocket

Preparation time: approx.
25 minutes (plus cooking time)
Per portion approx. 387 kcal/
1628 kJ
39 g P, 23 g F, 4 g CH

1 Sprinkle the plaice fillets with a little lemon juice, season with salt and pepper. Peel and finely dice the shallot. Clean and rinse the mushrooms, dry thoroughly and slice into strips.

2 Heat the butter and sauté the mushrooms. Fry the diced shallot with the mushrooms for approx. 5 minutes. Pour in the sherry and cook until the liquid has almost completely evaporated.

3 Stir in the crème fraîche and season all the ingredients with salt, pepper and the remaining lemon juice. Continue cooking for a further 5 minutes.

4 Clean, wash and spin-dry the rocket. Place 2 leaves on each plaice fillet. Roll up the fish fillets, tie the rolled-up plaice securely with kitchen twine and lay on top of the mushrooms. Cover and cook over a medium heat for approx. 10 minutes.

5 Shred the remaining rocket into strips. Once the fish is cooked, arrange the fish roulades and mushroom ragout on plates. Sprinkle with shredded rocket and serve.

Hake roulades
with bacon

Serves 4

4 pieces hake fillet (frozen)
lemon juice
8 rashers bacon
salt
pepper
3 tbsp clarified butter
250 ml fish stock
20 ml rum
5 tbsp mango chutney
2 tbsp Seville orange
marmalade
dill, lemon wedges and
lemon pepper to garnish

Preparation time: approx.
30 minutes
Per portion approx. 406 kcal/
1706 kJ
42 g P, 36 g F, 12 g CH

1 Defrost the fish, then wash, dry and sprinkle with lemon juice and top with bacon. Season with salt and pepper. Roll up the fish fillets and secure with wooden cocktail sticks.

2 Heat the clarified butter in a frying pan and sauté the fish rolls on all sides for approx. 6 minutes. Remove the fish from the pan and keep warm.

3 Add the fish stock to the cooking juices remaining in the frying pan and pour in the rum. Cook over a low heat for approx. 4 minutes to allow the flavours to blend.

4 Bring the stock to a boil and stir in the mango chutney and orange marmalade. Season all the ingredients with salt and pepper. Return the fish fillets to the pan.

5 Arrange the fish rolls on plates and drizzle the sauce over the top. Sprinkle a dusting of lemon pepper over the dish and garnish with wedges of lemon and a sprig of dill. Wild rice makes a perfect accompaniment to this dish.

Sole with
strawberry and pepper sauce

Serves 4

1 unwaxed lemon

4 sole fillets, ready to cook
(75–100 g each)

salt

50 g lean bacon

250 g strawberries

150 ml dry rosé wine

2 tsp cornstarch

125 ml fish or chicken stock

1 tsp preserved green
peppercorns

flour for coating

1 tbsp butter

lemon balm (rinsed) and a
few green peppercorns to
garnish

Preparation time: approx.
20 minutes (plus frying time)
Per portion approx. 214 kcal/
898 kJ
30 g P, 6 g F, 9 g CH

1 Wash the lemon in hot water, dry and finely grate about half the rind. Squeeze the juice from the lemon and sprinkle over the fish fillets. Lightly season the fish with salt and set aside.

2 Finely dice the bacon. Clean and wash the strawberries. Reserving 4 pieces of fruit, finely dice the rest. Mix a little of the wine and cornstarch together to form a smooth paste.

3 Combine the remaining wine with the stock, diced strawberries, lemon zest and pepper and simmer for approx. 5 minutes. Blend in the cornstarch mixture to thicken, then season with salt and keep warm.

4 Toss the sole fillets in flour. Heat the butter in a frying pan and fry the bacon until crisp. Remove from the pan and drain on paper kitchen towel. In the same fat, sauté the sole on both sides for 4 minutes.

5 Arrange the fish on plates, sprinkled with the crisp bacon and accompanied by a serving of sauce. Garnish with the reserved strawberries, a little lemon balm and a few green peppercorns before serving.

Caribbean
fish platter

Serves 4

2 small onions

1 garlic clove

salt

4 beef tomatoes

4 chilli peppers

1 bunch parsley

1 tbsp lemon juice

4 tbsp olive oil

2 redfish, ready to cook (500 g each)

½ tsp pepper

4 ripe bananas

sunflower oil for frying

lemon slices to garnish

Preparation time: approx. 15 minutes (plus grilling time)
Per portion approx. 518 kcal/ 2174 kJ
50 g P, 22 g F, 29 g CH

1 Peel the onions and garlic, slice the onions into wafer-thin rings. Crush the garlic with a pinch of salt.

2 Cut a cross in the tomato skins, plunge in boiling water, then peel and dice. Wash the peppers, cut out the stalk, remove the seeds, then chop finely. Wash the parsley, shake off any excess water and roughly chop. Place all the ingredients in a bowl along with the lemon juice and 2 tablespoons of olive oil, mix together, then leave to marinate.

3 Wash and dry the fish. Using a sharp knife, cut the fish in half lengthwise and season with pepper. Brush the fish fillets with the remaining olive oil and grill over a medium heat, or sauté in a frying pan until golden brown.

4 Peel the bananas and cut into chunks, approx. ½ cm thick. Lightly season the sliced banana with salt and fry for about 5 minutes in the heated sunflower oil until golden brown. Remove from the fat and drain on paper kitchen towel.

5 Arrange the banana slices and grilled fish on a platter. Garnish with the tomato-and-onion mixture and a few lemon slices, then serve immediately.

Fish shashlik
with garlic

Serves 4

400 g redfish fillet
200 ml lemon juice
240 g broccoli
salt
240 g button mushrooms
240 g cherry tomatoes
pepper
garlic powder
oregano
thyme
1 tbsp olive oil
2 tbsp vegetable stock
4 tbsp yoghurt
fresh herbs
140 g rice
360 g leaf spinach
120 g onions
2 garlic cloves
4 tbsp vinaigrette (ready-made)

Preparation time: approx.
45 minutes
Per portion approx. 352 kcal/
1474 kJ
28 g P, 8 g F, 41 g CH

1 Wash and dry the fish fillet, then cut into chunks approx. 2 x 2 cm. Sprinkle with lemon juice and allow to stand for a while.

2 Wash the broccoli and divide into florets, roughly similar in size. Cook in boiling, salted water for approx. 7 minutes until just firm to the bite.

3 Clean and wash the button mushrooms. Then, depending on their size, either leave them whole or cut into halves or quarters. Wash the cherry tomatoes.

4 Load metal or wooden skewers with alternating chunks of fish, tomatoes, broccoli and mushrooms. Season with salt and pepper, sprinkle with garlic, oregano and thyme and spray or brush with olive oil.

5 Sauté the fish kebabs on all sides in a non-stick frying pan for approx. 10 minutes. Add the vegetable stock to the cooking juices, stir in the yoghurt and season with salt, pepper, garlic powder and fresh herbs.

6 Cook the rice in salted water and drain in a sieve. Wash and pick over the spinach. Peel and very finely chop the onions. Peel and crush the garlic in a garlic press. Mix the onions and garlic with the vinaigrette and pour it over the spinach. Remove the fish kebabs from the frying pan and place on plates with a portion of rice. Serve with the accompanying sauce and spinach mixture.

Fish platter
with herb sauce

Serves 4

600 g spinach
2 garlic cloves
2 tbsp sunflower oil
300 g pollock fillet
juice of ½ lemon
salt
freshly ground pepper
200 g monkfish fillet
6 prawn tails
125 g butter
1 onion
250 ml dry white wine
250 ml vegetable stock
1 tsp tomato purée
pinch of cayenne pepper
2 bunches chopped dill
1 bunch chopped chives
freshly grated nutmeg
limes, bean sprouts and
chervil to garnish

Preparation time: approx.
30 minutes (plus cooking time)
Per portion approx. 348 kcal/
1460 kJ
41 g P, 14 g F, 7 g CH

1 Clean and wash the spinach. Peel and finely dice the garlic, then fry in 1 tablespoon of oil. Add the spinach, without shaking off any excess water. Cook with the garlic for 3 minutes, then keep warm.

2 Drizzle the lemon juice over the pollock, season with pepper and salt, then set aside. Slice the monkfish and season each side with pepper and salt. Cut through the prawn shells lengthwise, de-vein, wash and drain. Season lightly with salt and pepper.

3 Heat 3 tablespoons of butter with 1 tablespoon of oil in a frying pan. Sauté the fish and prawn tails in the hot fat, one after the other, for approx. 5 minutes on both sides. Remove from the pan and keep warm.

4 Peel and finely dice the onion, then sweat it in the fat left in the frying pan. Pour in the wine and stock, simmer until the liquid is reduced by half. Blend in the tomato purée, cayenne pepper and the remaining butter, cut into small pieces. Increase the heat and stir in the herbs. Season with salt and pepper.

5 Divide the spinach between 4 plates, then season with salt and nutmeg. Arrange the fish and prawns on top of the spinach and drizzle with sauce. Garnish with limes, bean sprouts and chervil before serving.

Salmon

with almond topping

Serves 4

4 salmon fillets, 125 g each
salt
pepper
1 lemon
100 g fine breadcrumbs
60 g ground almonds
130 g butter
300 ml fish stock
100 g prawns
20 g mustard seeds
2 tbsp cornstarch
2 tbsp almond leaves

Preparation time: approx.
25 minutes (plus frying time)
Per portion approx. 523 kcal/
2195 kJ
35 g P, 33 g F, 22 g CH

1 Rub the fish fillets with salt and pepper. Wash the lemon in hot water and cut into 8 segments.

2 Mix the breadcrumbs and ground almonds together. Spread the mixture over the top of the fish fillets.

3 Heat 30 g butter in a frying pan and sauté the salmon pieces in the hot fat, frying the coated side first, then turn and fry the other side.

4 To make the sauce, bring the fish stock to a boil in a saucepan. Chop the prawns and add to the stock along with the mustard seeds. Simmer until the mustard seeds turn soft. Stir the cornstarch into the sauce and add about 100 g butter, stirring constantly. Season to taste with salt and pepper.

5 Toast the almond leaves in a dry frying pan without fat, then sprinkle over the salmon fillets. Decorate with lemon wedges.

Salmon
with paprika topping

Serves 4

4 salmon fillets, 125 g each
salt
pepper
100 g fine breadcrumbs
2 tbsp mild paprika powder
130 g butter
300 ml fish stock
100 g prawns
20 g mustard seeds
2 tbsp cornstarch

Preparation time: approx.
25 minutes (plus frying time)
Per portion approx. 438 kcal/
1838 kJ
32 g P, 25 g F, 21 g CH

1 Pat the fish fillets dry and rub with salt and pepper.

2 Mix the breadcrumbs and paprika powder together. Rub this mixture into the top of the fish fillets.

3 Heat 30 g butter in a frying pan and sauté the salmon fillets, frying the side with the topping first, then turning over and cooking on the other side.

4 To make the sauce, bring the fish stock to a boil in a saucepan. Chop the prawns, then add to the stock with the mustard seeds. Simmer until the seeds turn soft. Stir the cornstarch into the liquid and add approx. 100 g butter, stirring constantly. Season to taste with salt and pepper.

5 Serve the salmon fillets with rice or potatoes.

Salmon
with dill and lemon

Serves 4

4 salmon fillets, 125 g each
salt
pepper
2 bunches dill
grated zest of 1 unwaxed lemon
100 g fine breadcrumbs
400 g beetroot
750 g potatoes
300 ml fish stock
100 g prawns
20 g mustard seeds
2 tbsp cornstarch
150 g butter

Preparation time: approx.
25 minutes (plus cooking time)
Per portion approx. 503 kcal/
2110 kJ
34 g P, 24 g F, 37 g CH

1 Pat the fish fillets dry using paper kitchen towel, then rub with salt and pepper. Finely chop the dill and mix with the lemon zest and breadcrumbs. Rub this mixture into the top side of the fish.

2 Cook the beetroot in their skins in salted water, then allow to cool. Peel and cook the potatoes.

3 To make the sauce, bring the fish stock to a boil in a saucepan. Chop the prawns and add to the stock along with the mustard seeds. Simmer until the mustard seeds have softened. Stir the cornstarch into the sauce and approx. 100 g butter, stirring constantly. Season with salt and pepper.

4 Peel and finely chop the beetroot. Heat 2 table-spoons of butter in a frying pan and briefly sauté the beetroot.

5 In another frying pan, heat the remaining butter and fry the salmon fillets, browning the bread-crumbed side first, then turning over and cooking on the other side.

6 Serve the salmon fillets with the sauce, beetroot and potatoes.

Fried sardines
with tomatoes and onions

Serves 4

600 g sardines

2 tbsp lemon juice

2 tins peeled plum tomatoes
(300 g each)

2 onions

4 tbsp oil

salt

pepper

sugar

1 tsp fennel seeds

2 tbsp flour

½ bunch flat-leaf parsley

Preparation time: approx.
25 minutes (plus cooking time)
Per portion approx. 275 kcal/
1155 kJ
31 g P, 12 g F, 10 g CH

1 Descale the sardines and cut off the dorsal fins. Gut the fish, rinse under cold, running water, then dry. Sprinkle the lemon juice over the fish.

2 Finely dice the tomatoes. Peel and finely dice the onions and fry in 1 tablespoon of oil until translucent. Add the tomatoes and their juice. Season with salt, pepper, sugar and fennel seeds, and simmer for approx. 10 minutes.

3 Season the sardines inside and out with salt, then coat in flour. Sauté the fish in the remaining oil for 2–3 minutes on each side.

4 Wash the parsley, shake dry and cut into strips. Arrange the sardines on the bed of tomatoes and onions. Sprinkle with parsley strips to serve.

Tip

Get your fishmonger to gut the fish for you so it is ready to cook.

Pan-fried stockfish
with olives and morel mushrooms

Serves 4

800 g stockfish

25 g dried mushrooms
(e.g. porcini and morels)

1 carrot

1 onion

2 garlic cloves

½ celery stick

3 tbsp olive oil

50 g pine kernels

200 ml dry white wine

salt

500 g potatoes

2 tbsp tomato purée

150 g black olives

Preparation time: approx.
30 minutes (plus time for soaking
and cooking)
Per portion approx. 855 kcal/
3591 kJ
124 g P, 27 g F, 25 g CH

1 Soak the fish in water for at least 2 days, then rinse thoroughly, pat dry with paper towel and cut into chunks. Soak the mushrooms in hot water for 30 minutes.

2 Peel the carrot, onion and garlic. Clean and wash the celery. Dice the vegetables and finely chop the garlic. Heat the olive oil in a frying pan and gently fry the vegetables and garlic together.

3 Drain the mushrooms, reserving the liquid, and finely chop the mushrooms.

4 Add the stockfish, mushrooms and pine kernels to the frying pan and continue cooking for 2 minutes, then pour in the wine and season the fish with salt.

5 Wash and peel the potatoes, then cut them into bite-sized chunks. Mix the tomato purée with 3 tablespoons of water, then add to the fish mixture along with the potatoes. Simmer all the ingredients for approx. 30 minutes. Mix in the pitted olives just before serving.

Fried sturgeon
with tomatoes

Serves 4

4 tbsp milk

salt

pepper

1 onion

6–8 tomatoes

500 g sturgeon fillet

flour

3 tbsp butter

parsley or dill

Preparation time: approx.
40 minutes
Per portion approx. 219 kcal/
919 kJ
30 g P, 7 g F, 9 g CH

1 Mix the milk with a pinch each of salt and pepper.

2 Peel the onion and slice into rings. Cut a cross in the tomato skins, douse with boiling water, peel, then cut in half.

3 Divide the fish fillet into portions and dip each one in the milk. Next, toss the fish in flour and fry in hot fat in a frying pan. Keep warm.

4 In a second frying pan, sprinkle the halved tomatoes with salt and pepper and fry for a few minutes.

5 Sweat the onion rings separately in hot fat until golden brown. Pour the cooking juices from the frying pan over the sturgeon fillets, sprinkle with fresh parsley or dill and serve on a warmed platter. Arrange a portion of halved tomatoes and onion rings on each plate.

Rhine pike
in sour cream

Serves 4

100 g streaky bacon
1 kg pike fillet
salt
juice of 1 lemon
20 g butter
500 ml dry white wine
250 ml vegetable stock
1 tbsp potato flour
300 g sour cream
pepper
1 tbsp capers

Preparation time: approx.
45 minutes
Per portion approx. 460 kcal/
1932 kJ
53 g P, 22 g F, 7 g CH

1 Cut the bacon into thin strips. Wash and dry the pike fillet, then dot the fillets with bacon. Season with salt and sprinkle with lemon juice.

2 Heat the butter in a frying pan and fry the fillets on both sides until browned. Pour in the wine and stock. Cover the pike fillets and poach over a low heat for about 15 minutes. Remove the pike fillets and keep warm.

3 Stir the potato flour to a smooth paste with the sour cream, then add to the fish stock and blend well. Bring the sauce to a boil, then season to taste with salt and pepper. Strain the sauce through a sieve and pour over the pike fillets. Finely chop the capers and sprinkle over the fish. Serve with boiled potatoes and cucumber salad.

Indian
halibut curry

Serves 4

1.2 kg halibut

salt

pepper

2 tbsp lemon juice

3 onions

6 tomatoes

2 tbsp oil

pinch of turmeric

2 tsp ground coriander

pinch of chilli powder

4 tbsp chopped coriander or
flat-leaf parsley

small amount of garam
masala (Indian spice
mixture, available from Asian
food stores)

Preparation time: approx.
15 minutes (plus cooking time)
Per portion approx. 338 kcal/
1418 kJ
62 g P, 6 g F, 7 g CH

1 Wash the fish and pat dry. Divide into 4 portion-sized pieces, season with salt and pepper, sprinkle with lemon juice and set aside.

2 Peel and finely chop the onions. Cut a cross in the tomato skins, douse with boiling water, then peel off the skins, remove the stalks and roughly chop.

3 Heat the oil in a frying pan and gently fry the onions for 2 minutes before stirring in the turmeric, coriander powder and chilli powder. Continue to cook until the mixture begins to release its aromas.

4 Add the fish, then the tomatoes and cook for approx. 3 minutes. Sprinkle all the ingredients with half the coriander or parsley and a little garam masala. Leave to marinate for 8–10 minutes.

5 Sprinkle the curry with the remaining coriander or parsley. Serve this dish with rice or Indian naan bread.

Tip

Halibut meat is light in colour with a good flavour but not quite as delicate as brill and turbot. Black Greenland halibut is more delicate in flavour than white halibut.

Oven-baked dishes

Ham-stuffed char

Serves 4

2 char, ready to cook
(800 g each)

juice of 1 lemon

salt

pepper

250 g cooked ham

1 green pepper

2 onions

100 g fine breadcrumbs
for coating

4 tbsp lemon juice

½ bunch dill

2 tbsp butter

Preparation time: approx.
25 minutes (plus cooking time)
Per portion approx. 343 kcal/
1438 kJ
42 g P, 9 g F, 22 g CH

1 Sprinkle the fish inside and out with lemon juice, then season with salt and pepper. Pre-heat the oven to 180 °C (Gas Mark 4).

2 Dice the cooked ham. Clean, de-seed and finely chop the green pepper. Peel and finely chop the onions. Combine with the pepper, breadcrumbs and lemon juice.

3 Finely chop the dill and add to the mixture. Stuff the fish with the ham filling and dot with butter.

4 Wrap the fish in greased aluminium foil and cook in the pre-heated oven for approx. 30 minutes.

Herb-stuffed char

Serves 4

2 char, ready to cook
(800 g each)

juice of 1 lemon

salt

pepper

1 onion

2 tbsp butter

1½ tsp each freshly chopped
thyme, marjoram, dill and
parsley

80 g fine breadcrumbs
for coating

Preparation time: approx.
25 minutes (plus cooking time)
Per portion approx. 315 kcal/
1323 kJ
41 g P, 9 g F, 17 g CH

1 Sprinkle the fish inside and out with lemon juice and rub with salt and pepper. Pre-heat the oven to 180 °C (Gas Mark 4).

2 Peel and chop the onion. Heat 1 tablespoon of butter in a frying pan and fry the onion until translucent. Add the herbs and breadcrumbs, and cook for a few more minutes.

3 Stuff the fish with this mixture, brush with the remaining butter, then roll up and secure well.

4 Wrap the fish in greased aluminium foil and bake in the pre-heated oven for about 30 minutes.

Char with
cheese and almond stuffing

Serves 4

2 char, ready to cook
(800 g each)

juice of 1 lemon

salt

pepper

1 bunch chervil

150 g butter cheese (ladies'
cheese)

2 slices white bread

2 tbsp chopped almonds

200 g crème fraîche

2 tsp mustard

3 tbsp butter

200 ml dry white wine

2 spring onions

Preparation time: approx.
30 minutes (plus baking time)
Per portion approx. 530 kcal/
2226 kJ
50 g P, 30 g F, 11 g CH

1 Sprinkle the fish inside and out with lemon juice, then rub with salt and pepper. Finely chop the chervil. Pre-heat the oven to 180 °C (Gas Mark 4).

2 Grate the butter cheese, remove the crusts from the white bread and cut into small cubes. In a bowl, combine the chervil (reserving 2 tablespoons), cheese, white bread and almonds.

3 Blend 3 tablespoons of crème fraîche and mustard together, stir into the cheese-and-almond mixture and stuff the fish with this filling. Close up the fish and secure with cocktail sticks.

4 Place the fish in a large, oiled roasting dish. Dot with butter, pour in the wine and bake the fish in a pre-heated oven for approx. 35 minutes.

5 Rinse and slice the spring onions into rings. Remove the fish from the roasting dish and keep warm. Drain off the liquid, top up with water to reach the 250 ml level. Stir in the rest of the crème fraîche.

6 Simmer the sauce until it has reduced somewhat, then season with salt and pepper. Add the spring onions and the rest of the chervil. Allow half a fish for each person and serve with a tomato salad.

Sea bass
with coriander

Serves 4

150 g butter

1.5 kg sea bass, ready to cook

4 onions

4 garlic cloves

4 tomatoes

2–4 sprigs fresh coriander

2–4 limes

130 ml dry white wine

salt

pepper

Preparation time: approx.
15 minutes (plus cooking time)
Per portion approx. 520 kcal/
2184 kJ
26 g P, 34 g F, 14 g CH

1 Pre-heat the oven to 220 °C (Gas Mark 7). Depending on the size of the fish, brush 1 or 2 sheets of aluminium foil generously with butter. Wash the fish, dry and place on the foil. Brush the fish with the remaining butter.

2 Peel and slice the onions and garlic. Cut a cross-shaped incision in the tomato skins, douse with boiling water, peel off the skins, de-seed and dice. Wash the coriander and shake dry.

3 Divide the vegetable and coriander between the fish. Cut the limes in half and squeeze out the juice. Sprinkle the fish with 8 tablespoons of lime juice and white wine. Season with salt and pepper.

4 Fold the aluminium foil over the fish and seal tightly. Bake the fish in the pre-heated oven for about 45 minutes. Serve the fish wrapped in foil. Rice makes an excellent accompaniment to this dish.

Tip

A useful rule of thumb when calculating the cooking time for the fish is to measure the thickest part of the fish, then reckon approx. 5 minutes per centimetre.

Oven-baked
rainbow trout

Serves 4

1 rainbow trout, ready to cook (approx. 1.5 kg)

1 tbsp lemon juice

salt

pepper

1 whole bunch celery

8 tomatoes

50 g 8-spice mixture (frozen)

80 g butter for grilling

20 ml whisky

Preparation time: approx. 20 minutes (plus cooking time)
Per portion approx. 485 kcal/ 2037 kJ
74 g P, 40 g F, 11 g CH

1 Pre-heat the oven to 180 °C (Gas Mark 4). Wash and dry the fish, then drizzle with lemon juice. Season with salt and pepper. Clean and wash the celery, then cut into pieces.

2 Clean and wash the tomatoes, cut in half, then into thin strips. Defrost the herbs, then mix 30 g herbs with the celery and tomatoes.

3 Stuff the trout with this mixture. Close the opening by securing with wooden cocktail sticks. Grease the aluminium foil with 20 g butter, lay the fish on the foil and drizzle with whisky. Dot the rest of the butter on the fish and sprinkle the remaining herbs on top.

4 Fold the short sides of the foil into the middle, then fold over the long sides. Bake the fish on the middle shelf of the pre-heated oven for approx. 20 minutes. Arrange on plates and serve with rice.

Provençal-style
monkfish

Serves 4

300 g green or wild asparagus

7 tbsp olive oil

6 garlic cloves

1 bunch dill

175 g black olives

2 tbsp breadcrumbs for coating

750 g monkfish fillet

salt

pepper

3–4 tbsp cold-pressed olive oil

Preparation time: approx. 20 minutes (plus frying time)

Per portion approx. 373 kcal/ 1565 kJ

31 g P, 25 g F, 7 g CH

1 Cut off the woody ends of the asparagus. Peel the lower third of the asparagus and cut into approx. 8-cm lengths. Pre-heat the oven to 225 °C (Gas Mark 7–8). Pour 4 tablespoons of olive oil into a baking dish and heat until hot.

2 Peel the garlic and grate into fine slices. Wash the dill and shake dry, then tear the leaves off the stems. Pit the olives and finely chop. Mix the olives with 3 tablespoons of olive oil and the breadcrumbs.

3 Separate the fish fillets from the backbone, then wash and pat dry. Season with salt and pepper. Place the fish and asparagus in the hot baking dish and bake in the pre-heated oven for approx. 5–6 minutes.

4 Switch the oven grill to 250 °C (Gas Mark 9) and spread the olive-and-breadcrumb mixture over the asparagus. Bake under the grill for approx. 3 minutes.

5 Sweat the garlic and dill briefly in olive oil. The garlic should not be allowed to brown otherwise it will develop a bitter taste. Arrange the Provençal-style monkfish on the bed of asparagus and serve drizzled with garlic-and-dill sauce.

Bacon-topped
pike

Serves 4

1 pike (approx. 1 kg)

100 g streaky bacon

salt

pepper

100 g butter

250 ml sour cream

1 tbsp tarragon vinegar

juice of ½ lemon

½ bunch dill

Preparation time: approx.
30 minutes (plus cooking time)
Per portion approx. 573 kcal/
2407 kJ
48 g P, 41 g F, 2 g CH

1 Gut and descale the pike, then wash well. Pat dry and, using a sharp knife, make incisions 3 cm apart on either side of the backbone. Cut the bacon into strips, then wedge into these slits in the pike flesh. Pre-heat the oven to 200 °C (Gas Mark 6).

2 Rub the fish with salt and pepper, bind the head and tail together. Melt the butter in a frying pan and cook the fish for about 25 minutes over a low heat, basting frequently with the butter.

3 Place the contents of the frying pan in an oven-proof baking dish, add the sour cream and cover the baking dish with aluminium foil. Bake in the pre-heated oven for a further 10 minutes.

4 Remove the pike from the baking dish and keep warm. Combine the sauce, vinegar and lemon juice. Wash the dill, shake dry and finely chop, then add to the sauce. Divide the pike into individual portions and serve with the sauce, potatoes and salad.

Oven-baked herrings
stuffed with onions

Serves 4

800 g fresh herring
juice of 1 lemon
1 tbsp salt
4 tbsp mild mustard
2 onions
fine breadcrumbs for coating
2 tbsp butter

Preparation time: approx.
30 minutes (plus baking time)
Per portion approx. 290 kcal/
1218 kJ
37 g P, 15 g F, 2 g CH

1 Pre-heat the oven to 225 °C (Gas Mark 6–7). Gut the herrings, remove the backbone, clean, rinse and drain. Sprinkle the inside of the fish with lemon juice and season with salt.

2 Spread 1 tablespoon of mustard on the inside of each herring. Peel and finely dice the onions. Stuff the cavity of each fish with diced onions and close up the herrings again. Coat the fish with breadcrumbs, pressing them gently into the skin. Grease an ovenproof baking dish with a little butter and arrange the herrings side by side.

3 Dot the remaining butter over the herrings. Bake in the pre-heated oven for 20–30 minutes. Boiled potatoes with peas and carrots make perfect partners for this dish.

Baked
carp

Serves 4

1 carp, ready to cook

salt

500 g potatoes

1 bunch spring onions

½ tsp mild paprika powder

150 g sour cream

20 g butter

fat for greasing the roasting dish

Preparation time: approx.
30 minutes (plus frying time)
Per portion approx. 413 kcal/
1733 kJ
31 g P, 23 g F, 20 g CH

1 Gut and fillet the carp, cut into chunks, then rub the fish with salt.

2 Wash, peel and thinly slice the potatoes. Clean and rinse the spring onions and slice into rings. Pre-heat the oven to 220 °C (Gas Mark 7). Grease a large roasting dish with butter.

3 Place half the spring onions in the tin, layer the potato slices on top and sprinkle with salt and a little paprika powder. Arrange the fish chunks on top of the potatoes and pour the sour cream over the top.

4 Sprinkle the remaining spring onions and paprika powder over the top and dot with butter. Bake the carp in the pre-heated oven for approx. 60 minutes. Serve in the roasting dish.

Foil-wrapped gurnard

Serves 4

8 baby potatoes
2 onions
2 tomatoes
2 lemons
4 gurnards, ready to cook
(approx. 200 g each)
oil for greasing the foil
salt
pepper
chilli powder
2 bay leaves
1 garlic clove
1 bunch flat-leaf parsley

Preparation time: approx.
20 minutes (plus baking time)
Per portion approx. 530 kcal/
2226 kJ
45 g P, 6 g F, 68 g CH

1 Wash and thoroughly brush the baby potatoes. Cook briefly in their skins in boiling water, then plunge in cold water and allow to cool, then peel and cut in half.

2 Peel and slice the onions into rings. Wash the tomatoes, cut out the stalks and slice. Peel and slice the lemons. Wash and dry the fish. Pre-heat the oven to 200 °C (Gas Mark 6).

3 Brush 4 large pieces of extra strong aluminium foil with oil. Lay the fish on the foil and cover each one with one quarter of the tomato, lemon and onion slices. Arrange the potato halves around the fish.

4 Season all the ingredients with salt, pepper and chilli powder and place half a bay leaf on each fish. Peel and very finely chop the garlic and sprinkle over the fish. Wash the parsley and shake dry, then chop finely before sprinkling it over the fish.

5 Fold the foil into a parcel and bake the fish in the pre-heated oven for about 35 minutes. Serve the fish in their foil parcels and unwrap at the table.

Fish goulash
with potatoes

Serves 4

1 sturgeon, ready to cook
(approx. 1 kg)

4 potatoes

1 onion

½ tsp mild paprika powder

3 tbsp sour cream

100 g freshly grated Gruyère

20 g butter

fine breadcrumbs for coating

150 g cream

fat for greasing the baking
dish

Preparation time: approx.
30 minutes (plus cooking time)
Per portion approx. 548 kcal/
2299 kJ
55 g P, 28 g F, 19 g CH

1 Prepare the fish, then slice into thick chunks.
Cook the fish in a saucepan for about 5 minutes
in lightly salted water. Remove the fish pieces from
the pan and allow to cool. Next, skin the fish and
remove the bones. Cut the fish into bite-sized pieces.

2 Wash the potatoes and cook in boiling water for
about 20 minutes. Drain and leave to cool for a
while, then peel and thinly slice. Peel and chop the
onion. Pre-heat the oven to 220 °C (Gas Mark 7).

3 Grease a baking dish and layer the sliced potatoes over the base of the dish. Spread the
onions, paprika powder and sour cream over the
potatoes, then arrange the fish pieces on the bed of
vegetables and sprinkle with the grated Gruyère
cheese. Finally, dot butter over the top and sprinkle
with breadcrumbs.

4 Pour the cream over the fish ragout and bake in
the pre-heated oven for about 40 minutes.
Serve in the baking dish whilst still hot.

Baked

freshwater whitefish

Serves 4

800 g whitefish fillets, skinned and boned

juice of 1 lemon

2 carrots

1 celery stick

2 tbsp butter

salt

pepper

200 ml cream

small amount of dill to garnish

fat for greasing the baking dish

Preparation time: approx. 20 minutes (plus cooking time)
Per portion approx. 425 kcal/ 1785 kJ
45 g P, 25 g F, 5 g CH

1 Wash the fish fillets and pat dry. Sprinkle with lemon juice and set aside.

2 Pre-heat the oven to 180 °C (Gas Mark 4). Peel and slice the carrots. Clean, wash and thinly slice the celery.

3 Heat 1 tablespoon of butter in a frying pan, then cook the carrots and celery in the melted fat for about 3 minutes. Season with salt and pepper.

4 Grease a baking dish and spread the vegetables across the base of the dish. Season the fish fillets with salt and pepper, and lay them on the bed of vegetables. Melt the remaining butter and drizzle over the fish.

5 Place the baking dish in the pre-heated oven. After approx. 5 minutes, pour the cream over the fish fillets and cook for a further 15 minutes in the oven. Serve the whitefish fillets garnished with dill and with an accompaniment of rice or potatoes.

Cheese-topped salmon
with chard

Serves 4

butter for greasing the
baking dish

500 g tagliatelle

800 g chard

salt

2 onions

1 garlic clove

4 pieces of fresh salmon
(150 g each)

juice and zest of 1 unwaxed
lemon

pepper

150 g fresh, peeled prawns

150 g mozzarella

2 tbsp olive oil

grated nutmeg

Preparation time: approx.
20 minutes (plus cooking time)
Per portion approx. 485 kcal/
2037 kJ
62 g P, 24 g F, 90 g CH

1 Grease a baking dish. Pre-heat the oven to 225 °C
(Gas Mark 7–8). Cook the pasta in salted water
according to the instructions on the packet until just
firm to the bite.

2 Wash the chard and remove the leaves from the
stems. Cut the green chard leaves into broad
strips and the stems into thin strips. Peel and finely
dice the onions and garlic.

3 Sprinkle the salmon with lemon juice, season
with salt and pepper, and sprinkle the grated
lemon zest over the top. Rinse the prawns and pat
dry. Cut the mozzarella into slices.

4 Heat the oil in a large saucepan, then sweat the
onions in the oil until translucent. Add the
chard stems and garlic, season with salt, pepper and
nutmeg, then cook for approx. 5 minutes. Add the
chard leaves to the other ingredients and cook for
about 3 more minutes.

5 Mix the chard-and-onion mixture with the tagliatelle and tip into the greased baking dish.

6 Arrange the salmon and prawns on the bed of
pasta, place the mozzarella slices over the top
and bake the salmon gratin in the pre-heated oven
for approx. 15 minutes. Serve in the baking dish.

Stockfish in tomato and wine sauce

Serves 4

750 g stockfish
400 g shallots
1 whole garlic
750 g tomatoes
1 unwaxed lemon
125 g black olives
1 tin chick peas (drained weight approx. 240 g)
salt
pepper
3 bay leaves
100 ml dry red wine
8 tbsp olive oil

Preparation time: approx.
15 minutes (plus soaking and cooking time)
Per portion approx. 950 kcal/
3990 kJ
149 g P, 28 g F, 21 g CH

1 Divide the stockfish into smaller pieces, then soak in plenty of cold water for 2 days, changing the water several times during the process. Drain off the water, skin and bone the fish and cut into large chunks.

2 Pre-heat the oven to 225 °C (Gas Mark 7–8). Peel the shallots and rinse the garlic. Make an incision in the tomato skins, douse with boiling water, then peel off the skins and cut in half. Cut out the stalks and roughly chop the tomatoes.

3 Wash and slice the lemon. Drain the olives and chick peas.

4 In a baking dish, arrange alternating layers of fish, shallots, tomatoes, olives, chick peas and lemon slices, seasoning each layer with salt and pepper. Insert the whole garlic and bay leaves between the layers and sprinkle a little salt and pepper over the top.

5 Pour in the wine and olive oil. Cover the baking dish with a tight-fitting lid and bake in the pre-heated oven for approx. 50 minutes.

Sardines

stuffed with spinach

Serves 4

700 g sardines, heads
removed and ready to cook

1 day-old bread roll

250 g spinach

2 garlic cloves

½ bunch of basil

1 egg

40 g grated Parmesan

salt

pepper

4 tbsp olive oil

1 tbsp pine kernels

oil for greasing the baking
dish

Preparation time: approx.
25 minutes (plus baking time)
Per portion approx. 498 kcal/
2090 kJ
45 g P, 32 g F, 8 g CH

1 Wash the sardines and pat dry. Soak the bread roll in warm water. Clean and wash the spinach, blanch in boiling, salted water for approx. 2 minutes. Pour off the water and allow to drain.

2 Pre-heat the oven to 240 °C (Gas Mark 9). Peel and chop the garlic, wash the basil and shake dry, then finely chop. Squeeze the excess water from the bread. Chop the spinach and mix with the garlic, basil, bread roll, egg and Parmesan until it forms a compact mass. Season with salt and pepper.

3 Stuff the sardines with the spinach mixture, then arrange them in a large, greased, baking dish and drizzle with olive oil. Sprinkle the pine kernels over the top. Bake in the pre-heated oven for about 15 minutes.

Spicy stuffed mussels

Serves 4

1.5 kg mussels

5 eggs

250 g fine breadcrumbs
for coating

125 g freshly grated
Pecorino

3 tbsp freshly chopped
parsley

1 garlic clove

3 tbsp olive oil

400 g puréed tomatoes

salt

pepper

1 tbsp freshly chopped
oregano

Preparation time: approx.
30 minutes (plus baking time)
Per portion approx. 768 kcal/
3224 kJ
60 g P, 30 g F, 64 g CH

1 Thoroughly rinse and brush the mussels under running water, discarding any which are not fully closed. Pre-heat the oven to 200 °C (Gas Mark 6). Bring the water to a boil in a large saucepan and cook the mussels for approx. 5 minutes until they have all opened. Any which have not opened during cooking should be discarded. Drain the mussels.

2 Lightly beat the eggs and combine with the breadcrumbs and cheese. Stir in the parsley and whisk all the ingredients to a creamy consistency. Place the opened mussels on a baking sheet and spread the egg mixture over the top. Carefully close up the mussel shells and bake in the pre-heated oven for approx. 15 minutes.

3 To make the sauce, peel and finely chop the garlic. Heat the oil in a saucepan and gently fry the garlic. Add the tomatoes and simmer the mixture for about 10 minutes over a moderate heat. Season with salt, pepper and oregano.

4 Divide the sauce between 4 plates and arrange the mussels on top. Serve with an accompaniment of rice.

Lobster Newburg

Serves 4

2 frozen lobsters, 600 g each
salt
juice of ½ lemon
3 chopped onions
80 g butter
125 ml cream
1 tbsp cornstarch
3 tbsp sherry
4 egg yolks
pepper
150 g button mushrooms
40 g freshly grated cheese

Preparation time: approx.
35 minutes (plus cooking time)
Per portion approx. 475 kcal/
1995 kJ
62 g P, 22 g F, 6 g CH

1 Pre-heat the oven to 250 °C (Gas Mark 9). Defrost the lobsters, then cook until tender for 15 minutes in 750 ml salted, boiling water. Remove the lobsters from the pan, drain and cut in half.

2 Crack open the shells and scoop out the meat. Do the same with the tail and claws. Drizzle lemon juice over the lobster meat and reserve the shells.

3 Melt a small amount of butter in a saucepan and sweat the onions. Stir the cream and cornstarch into a smooth paste, add to the pan, then bring to a boil, stirring constantly, and simmer for 3 minutes. Remove the sauce from the heat and blend in the egg yolks, which have been mixed with the sherry. Season with salt and pepper. Do not allow the sauce to boil again.

4 Clean and slice the mushrooms, then fry for 5 minutes in a small amount of butter. Carefully stir the mushrooms into the sauce along with the lobster meat. Avoid stirring to prevent the lobster falling apart.

5 Spoon the cooked mixture into the lobster shells, place on a greased baking sheet and sprinkle with cheese. Bake in the pre-heated oven for approx. 15 minutes. Freshly made buttered toast makes a perfect accompaniment to this dish.

Prawn quiche
with fennel

Serves 6

125 g butter
250 g flour
salt
1 bunch spring onions
1 fennel bulb
3 tomatoes
1 bunch dill
400 g North Sea prawns,
ready to cook
1 tbsp lemon juice
4 eggs
150 g cream
freshly ground white pepper
flour for rolling out the
pastry

Preparation time: approx.
20 minutes (plus chilling and
baking time)
Per portion approx. 513 kcal/
2155 kJ
24 g P, 31 g F, 35 g CH

1 Cut the butter into small pieces, then mix with the flour, a pinch of salt and about 3 tablespoons of cold water. Knead the ingredients into a smooth dough. Cover the dough with foil and chill in the refrigerator for about 30 minutes.

2 Clean and wash the spring onions, then finely chop. Clean and wash the fennel, then slice into fine strips. Make an incision in the tomato skins, douse with boiling water, then skin and finely chop the tomatoes. Wash, dry and finely chop the dill.

3 Pre-heat the oven to 200 °C (Gas Mark 6). Dust a work surface with a little flour, then roll out ⅔ of the pastry dough and line the base of a circular, springform baking tin. Use the remainder of the pastry to make a 3-cm wide strip to form the edge of the quiche.

4 Combine the vegetables with the dill and prawns, reserving a few sprigs of dill for the garnish. Stir in the lemon juice. Tip the mixture into the baking tin and spread evenly.

5 Mix the eggs and cream together and pour the mixture over the ingredients in the pastry case. Season with salt and pepper. Bake the quiche in the pre-heated oven for about 35 minutes until golden brown. Slice the quiche into individual portions, garnish with the remaining dill and serve.

Seafood gratin

Serves 4

1 kg mussels
750 ml vegetable stock
1 bunch spring onions
80 g butter
90 g flour
250 ml fish stock
250 ml cream
2 tbsp Worcester sauce
salt
pepper
250 g cooked prawn meat
3 tbsp freshly chopped parsley
150 g fine breadcrumbs for coating
fat for greasing

Preparation time: approx.
30 minutes (plus time for soaking and cooking)
Per portion approx. 708 kcal/ 2972 kJ
36 g P, 40 g F, 53 g CH

1 Thoroughly brush the mussels and remove any remnants of seaweed. Discard any mussels which are still open. Soak the mussels for about 30 minutes.

2 Heat the vegetable stock in a large saucepan and boil the mussels for about 6–8 minutes. Remove the shellfish from the stock and discard any mussels which have remained closed.

3 Scrape the mussels from their shells. Clean and slice the spring onions into rings.

4 Melt the butter in a frying pan, stir in the flour, then pour in the fish stock and cream. Stirring constantly, simmer until the mixture is reduced in quantity and develops a creamy consistency. Season with Worcester sauce, salt and pepper. Stir in the prawns, parsley and breadcrumbs.

5 Lightly grease a baking dish. Add the mussels and top with the prawn and cream mixture. Place under a hot grill and bake for about 2–3 minutes until golden brown. Serve with a green salad.

Mediterranean-style
stuffed squid

Serves 4

1.2 kg fresh squid
juice of 1 lemon
salt
pepper
1 onion
1 garlic clove
150 g button mushrooms
3 tbsp olive oil
150 g minced beef
10 black olives, pitted
2 eggs
50 g fine breadcrumbs for
coating
40 g freshly grated Pecorino
2 tbsp mixed, chopped herbs
(parsley. thyme, basil)

Preparation time: approx.
45 minutes (plus baking time)
Per portion approx. 705 kcal/
2961 kJ
65 g P, 40 g F, 21 g CH

1 Wash the squid in running water. Peel off the thin layer of skin from the body, pull out the innards and tentacles from the main body. Using a sharp knife, cut off the innards and head and discard. Reserve the tentacles. Next, turn the squid inside out, wash again, then pat dry. Rub the squid with the juice of ½ lemon. Rub with lemon and turn again. Rub the outside with salt and pepper.

2 Cut the tentacles into small sections and boil for approx. 15 minutes in salted water with the rest of the lemon juice. Peel and chop the onion and garlic clove. Clean and wipe the mushrooms, then finely chop.

3 Heat 1 tablespoon of olive oil in a frying pan and sweat the onion and garlic. Add the minced beef and mushrooms and fry all the ingredients for about 5 minutes. Slice the olives and add to the meat mixture.

4 Pre-heat the oven to 180 °C (Gas Mark 4). In a bowl, combine the cooked tentacles with the eggs, breadcrumbs, meat-and-mushroom mixture, cheese and herbs. Season with salt and pepper.

5 Stuff the squid with this mixture and close up the openings with kitchen twine or a roulade pin. Grease a baking dish with olive oil and place the squid in the dish. Bake in the pre-heated oven for about 30 minutes, then place under the grill for a few minutes. Allow to cool. Before serving, cut into sections 2 cm thick. Serve with tomato sauce as an accompaniment.

Fish casserole
with potatoes

Serves 4

400 g potatoes
200 g carrots
1 leek
4 pike fillets
salt
2 tbsp oil
100 ml white wine
1 bunch dill
pepper
200 g sour cream
1 tbsp tomato purée
oil for greasing the baking dish

Preparation time: approx.
30 minutes (plus baking time)
Per portion approx. 308 kcal/
1291 kJ
33 g P, 9 g F, 20 g CH

1 Peel and slice the potatoes. Peel and slice the carrots. Clean the leek and slice into thin rings.

2 Pre-heat the oven to 175 °C (Gas Mark 4). Rub the fish fillets with salt and cut into fairly large pieces.

3 Grease a baking dish and fill with alternating layers of fish, potatoes, carrots and leek. Drizzle 2 tablespoons of oil over the top and pour in the wine.

4 Wash the dill, shake dry and chop. Sprinkle the casserole with dill, salt and pepper and bake in the pre-heated oven for about 35 minutes.

5 Mix the tomato purée with the sour cream and serve as an accompaniment to the casserole.

Index

Asparagus and zander in puff pastry 64

Bouillabaisse, French 107
Bream on a bed of mixed vegetables 129

Carp, baked 212
Carp goulash with peppers and sour cream 142
Carp, sweet-and-sour 151
Catfish with potato and wild garlic salad 163
Char with cheese-and-almond stuffing 200
Char, ham-stuffed 196
Char, herb-stuffed 199
Clam chowder 131
Cod, poached with horseradish 136
Cod with mustard-and-herb sauce 135
Crab soup, rich, with sherry 104

Eel kebabs with spicy dressing 80

Fish and seafood kebabs 83
Fish cakes with herbs 144
Fish casserole with potatoes 236
Fish goulash with potatoes 216
Fish in batter 156
Fish in red curry sauce 155

Fish platter, Caribbean 173
Fish platter with herb sauce 176
Fish shashlik with garlic 174
Fish soup, creamy, with tomatoes 109
Fish soup, sweet-and-sour, with glass noodles 103
Fish stew with herbs 141

Garlic prawn kebabs 51
Gurnard, foil-wrapped 214

Hake roulades with bacon 168
Halibut curry, Indian 193
Herring salad with beetroot 33
Herring salad with bacon and onions 89
Herrings, oven-baked, stuffed with onions 211
Herrings, pickled, with aquavit 22
Herrings, pickled, with ginger 24
Herrings, pickled, with tomatoes 21
Herrings, sweet-and-sour 18

Lobster Newburg 228
Lobster salad with mint 40

Marinated herring nibbles with paprika 44
Monkfish, Provençal-style 206

Mussel soup, creamy with smoked bacon	100
Mussel vol-au-vents	63
Mussels, Corsican-style	132
Mussels, Rhenish-style	29
Mussels, spicy, stuffed	226
Nigiri sushi with tuna and caviar	78
Oysters, grilled	71
Paella marinara	148
Perch, fried, with red curry and lychees	116
Pike, bacon-topped	208
Pike, Rhine, in sour cream	190
Plaice	152
Plaice roulades with rocket	167
Prawn parcels with hoisin sauce	72
Prawn quiche with fennel	231
Prawns in spicy sauce	27
Rainbow trout, oven-baked	205
Red snapper in banana leaf	122
Salmon and prawn terrines with fresh dill	17
Salmon, cheese-topped, with chard	221
Salmon kebabs, with vegetables	164
Salmon, marinated	36
Salmon-stuffed vine leaves	48
Salmon stuffed with crab meat	77
Salmon with almond topping	179
Salmon with dill and lemon	182
Salmon with dill and mustard sauce	52
Salmon with honey-and-dill sauce	57
Salmon with paprika topping	181
Salmon with vinaigrette dressing	54
Sardines, fried, with tomatoes and onions	184
Sardines stuffed with spinach	225
Sashimi with soy sauce	58
Savoy cabbage roulades with langoustines	84
Scallop salad with porcini mushrooms	15
Scallops, fried, with spring onions	124
Scallops, grilled	60
Scones with trout fillet	68
Sea bass with coriander	202
Sea bream, sweet-and-sour, with leek and carrot strips	126
Seafood gratin	233
Seafood, mixed, in ginger stock	96
Seafood salad with cashew nuts	30
Smoked salmon rolls with carrot spirals	34
Sole roulades with raisins	43
Sole with strawberry-and-pepper sauce	170
Spicy pollock and coconut soup	92
Squid, barbecued	86
Squid, stuffed, Asian-style	138
Squid, stuffed, Mediterranean-style	234
Stockfish in tomato and red wine sauce	222

Stockfish, pan-fried, with olives and morel
   mushrooms   186
Sturgeon, fried, with tomatoes   189
Swimmer crabs with curry sauce
   and coriander   99

Trout au bleu   119
Trout meunière   121
Trout tartare on rye bread   66
Tuna carpaccio with sherry   39
Tuna goulash with paprika   110
Turbot carpaccio in stock   95
Two-fish terrine   74

Whitefish, baked   219
Whitefish, freshwater, pan-fried   159
Whitefish with cream sauce   160

Zander curry with water chestnuts   114